READING
THE BOOK

. . . .

Reading
The
Book

....

Making the Bible a Timeless Text

BURTON L. VISOTZKY

*With a new foreword
by the author*

2005 • 5765
THE JEWISH PUBLICATION SOCIETY
Philadelphia

The Jewish Publication Society
2100 Arch Street, 2nd floor
Philadelphia, PA 19103

The Library of Congress has cataloged the cloth edition of this
book as:
Visotzky, Burton L.
    Reading the Book· making the Bible a timeless text / Burton
L. Visotzky
p. cm.
With a new foreword by the author.
ISBN 0-8276-0786-5 (JPS pbk.)
ISBN 0-8052-1072-5 (pbk.)
    1. Bible. O.T. Genesis —Criticism, interpretation, etc..
Jewish. 2. Midrash— History and criticism 1 Title
BS1235.2 V58 1996 96-17783
220.6'1   dc20   CIP

Manufactured in the United States of America

CONTENTS

	Foreword	vii
ONE	"Princess Di Delivers Two-headed Monster": Scripture and its Interpretation	1
TWO	God Dictates, Moses Composes	21
THREE	Rabbis as Readers	40
FOUR	Father Abraham, Teacher of Faith	57
FIVE	Binding Isaac	76
SIX	Jacob and Sons	100
SEVEN	Joseph's Bones	121
EIGHT	Dying	141
NINE	Siblings	160
TEN	Adam and Eve Back Together Again	183
ELEVEN	The Architecture of the Universe	204
TWELVE	Reading the Book	225

FOREWORD

When Umberto Eco wrote *The Name of the Rose*, he
called his work "a palimpsest." That is, a text written over
another text. I can think of no keener designation for
midrash, which is written—if we may imagine a heavenly
copy of the Torah (Written and Oral)—between the lines
of the written text, betwixt each word, around each letter,
interwoven with the calligraphic adornments, dotting the
vowel signs, over the still faintly visible letters of the earlier
words inscribed on the parchment so many centuries ago.
As the Rabbis of old would have it, the words of midrash
were given to Moses as God dictated the Torah at Mount
Sinai, the echo of every divine utterance resounding generations into the future, keeping the Revelation ever in the
present.

This book is a rabbi's romp through the art of his ancient
forebears, an introduction to midrash. By midrash I refer to
a specific process of reading Scripture and the literature
which that reading yields. Ancient, classical, rabbinic midrash
was an attempt by the Rabbis of the first few centuries
of the Common Era to reread the Bible in their own image.
They read the text assuming it spoke to them, in their

own era. The anthologies of these imaginative readings of Scripture span more than a millennium and are collectively called midrash. The Rabbis of old were fond of analogies, puns, king parables and anachronisms. In this book, I too delight in viewing the biblical text from odd angles, and in doing midrash on the ancient midrash itself until it speaks to us in a late-twentieth-century voice.

Others besides us midrash scholars have hearkened to the voice of the ancient Rabbis. Midrashic method has captured the fancy of literary critics, particularly the postmodernists— those obfuscating deconstructionists whom Professor Susan Handelman calls "slayers of Moses." Searching through the rubble of the past for a usable history to buttress their reading strategies, they have happily settled on midrash as a suitable ancestor, an ancient reading method that foretells their own contortions of the text. So midrash has been rediscovered and brought out to charm the literati, despite the fact that the most basic of reading assumptions, the very hermeneutic foundations on which the two disciplines rest, diverge a sharp 180 degrees one from the other.

For the deconstructionist, the text has no meaning but that which the critic imputes to it. The process of agonizing over the words is what forces them to yield meaning. The critic is all, while the author vanishes well below the literary horizon. Not so with midrash. For the Rabbis of old, the Author's intent was everything; it imbued the text with layers of richness beyond imagination. What was dictated by God at Sinai was all meaning, merely waiting for the critic to uncover it centuries hence. Like that of a diamond cutter, the job of the midrashist was to expose yet one more facet of the endless faces of Torah. Within the gem of Scripture still burned the fires and lightnings of the Revelation at Sinai. Midrash gives us a glimpse, a new glance at the illumination, at the brilliance lying within.

Yet, to be fair, the ancient midrashist brought contemporary tools to the text, much as does the postmodern deconstructionist. Whether those tools are the hermeneutics of the Alexandrian hellenists or the strategies of the American university, midrash decodes the divine Document for its own time, in its own day, as though the Words of God were always waiting to be heard. Like a whisper uttered long ago, it reaches the ear of a listener and brings clarity to his or her countenance.

The "her" of the last sentence is another recent addition to the norm of midrashic reading. In the good old days, the good ol' boys read midrash and Scripture in a rather exclusive club (no women, thank you). Today, millennia later, some of the most insightful midrash is being created through the happy vehicle of feminist readings of the Bible. My colleague and neighbor Professor Phyllis Trible, a Baptist, a feminist and a formidable reader of Scripture, has produced and inspired some of the profoundest midrash in this century. An entire generation of midrashists follows in her wake.

There are yet other means of making the Bible a timeless text. Some years ago, upon my return from a sabbatical year in Oxbridge, my interest in the midrashic process was sufficiently piqued that I undertook a long-running experiment. I had thought that if I gathered together a group of Bible scholars to read with a group of creative readers and writers, I might gain a clue as to how the Rabbis of old read Scripture. At my home institution, the Jewish Theological Seminary of America in New York City, I convened the Genesis Seminar with the goal of learning how midrash was achieved.

The seminar, which I describe briefly in Chapter Twelve, met monthly for five years, during which time we read our way through the fifty chapters of the Book of Genesis. Not a little midrash was created during those sessions in which screenwriters, poets, novelists, editors and essayists argued and discussed Scripture with Bible scholars, ministers and rabbis. We created modern midrash, a rereading of the Bible as it spoke to our twentieth-century consciousness. What was, perhaps, unusual about this midrash was that it came from such a mixed group: men and women, scoffers and believers, Jews, Christians and neither of the above (one Hindu Brahmin and one Zoroastrian were among us). What we shared was a commitment to the text, even though not all of us held it to be sacred or canonical. We also learned how to read the rough-and-tumble contextual meaning of Genesis, to recapture its "literal" meaning, and then start the midrashic process anew.

Throughout the half decade we spent reading together, the writers of the Genesis Seminar repeatedly asked me to teach them classical rabbinic midrash. I resisted doing so in our study groups because I was more interested in what they had to say about Genesis than in what my Rabbis of old had already said. But in my last year with the seminar, I began writing this book. I felt that I should give them ancient midrash—not only my writers' group but as broad an audience as possible. The Rabbis of old had lots of entertaining, creative and thought-provoking insights into the Scriptural text. They also had a unique way of reading, one which I thought worth introducing to a wide popular readership.

Having finished the Book of Genesis with my Genesis Seminar, I announced to the group of writers that it was time to move on, to close up shop. In the end, I moved on and they continue to study. I believe they are now reading the biblical books of Samuel. It pleases me very much that my study group has endured. I am equally pleased that *Reading the Book* has endured. I hope that through it readers will find their way to Bible or midrash study beyond these pages.

When I moved on, it was to continue the study of Genesis, but with different company. For the last four years I have read Genesis with two different groupings, each of which has given me insight and community in very satisfying ways. For the first, I formed a group much like my Genesis Seminar but consisting of CEOs, bankers and lawyers. This group met for two years at Kekst and Company on Madison Avenue, and then, somewhat reconstituted, in the boardroom of the Milstein Properties Offices in midtown Manhattan. The writers' seminar and the CEO seminar differed radically from each other. Indeed, although both groups were reading Genesis and the words remained the same, I sometimes wondered if each were not reading a different book after all.

Writers and CEOs simply view the world differently. Of course, this comes as no news, but it effectively illuminated for me an old saw about how a reading environment affects one's understanding of a book. Indeed, I find that virtually every time I reread Genesis I read it as a new book—for I have changed from year to year. This held true as well in my second reading venue, a television series that I had the good fortune of filming with Bill Moyers for PBS. I enjoyed immensely the many hours I spent with Bill and Company wrestling over the words of Genesis. Once again, it seemed a new book. Once again, we formed a close community who shared a commitment to the text. The resulting series, "Genesis: A Living Conversation," is set to premiere in October 1996.

Most recently, I turned my attention to a new book of my own: not about classical rabbinic midrash, but about contemporary midrash, modern readings of Genesis. That book, *The Genesis of Ethics* (Crown, 1996), is a study group on the page, a dialogue with the reader about the First Book of Moses. In it I try to share what I have learned in all of the study groups I have been privileged to lead and take part in during the past decade. The conclusions of our years of study as well as the methods of our conversation are represented there.

Sometimes I feel that every act of reading we do is midrash. And yet, midrash in its formal sense belongs to a certain time and place and, even more, to the Book of Books, the Bible. Midrash is an act of reading that makes the Bible a timeless text. It is an ancient literature with an unfamiliar method of reading. It is a culture that is at once similar to and alien from our own. To understand midrash one requires a sympathetic guide. I pray that *Reading the Book* can be that guide. I wrote it so that modern readers can share the joy I find in reading an ancient literature that itself takes great joy in Bible study. I introduce this book, then, as I close it, with the words of a wise Rabbi from ancient times: "Go now. Study."

New York
April 1996

READING
THE BOOK

. . . .

Chapter One

"PRINCESS DI DELIVERS TWO-HEADED MONSTER"

SCRIPTURE AND ITS INTERPRETATION

It just sits there on the shelf. Perhaps you got it for your bar mitzvah or christening, perhaps it was a wedding gift. Maybe you actually lifted it from a hotel room and took it home with you. Perhaps you even bought it with the best of intentions. It could be leather-bound with gilt letters, cloth-bound, or even a paperback. It might be the Hebrew Bible, the Torah of the Jews. Again, it might be the Old Testament with Apocrypha or the Testaments Old and New. Jews read it, Christians read it, even Muslims know of it. It's a favorite in Introduction to Literature courses and, of course, intro courses in Western religions. People on the subways often read it, carefully covered in plastic, all the while moving their lips. It's a bestseller—it doubtless always has been. But it just sits there on the shelf, inert, closed, silent. Go ahead, open it, read a Word or two.

What is it about the Bible that makes it so popular, so inspiring to some, while for others of us it remains a closed book? True, its phrases and cadences, especially in the King James version, grace the great works of the English language. But taken in its context, the prose itself is odd, hardly the same as King James's English when read in the original Hebrew or, even more so, in Greek. St. Jerome, among the greatest of translators of Scripture and certainly one of its greatest promoters, in a letter written in 384 baldly characterized the writing style as "rude and repellent." But Jerome also gives us the clue to its enormous popularity: it is a book which by communal consent admits of constant interpretation.

It is this ongoing interpretive engagement with the Book that evokes its popularity. As Jerome told Paulinus of Nola at the end of the fourth century, "You can make no progress in the Holy Scriptures unless you have a guide to show you the way." But St. Jerome knows that reading the Book can be a tricky enterprise; not all interpretation is admissible. He complains to Paulinus by quoting Horace: "Doctors alone profess the healing art, and none but joiners ever try to join." But, Jerome goes on, "the art of interpreting the Scriptures is the only one of which all men everywhere claim to be masters.
. . . The chatty old woman, the doting old man, and the worldly sophist, one and all take in hand the Scriptures, rend them in pieces and teach them before they have learned them."

Jerome's explanation for this tendency is straightforward:

> Genesis, we are told, needs no explanation; its topics are too simple—the birth of the world, the origin of the human race.
> . . . Exodus, no doubt, is equally plain; . . . the meaning of Leviticus is of course self-evident, . . . the book of Numbers too; . . . Deuteronomy also. . . . So far the "five words" of the Pentateuch.

St. Jerome's sarcasm is not lost on us in the twentieth century, when the "simple topics" of Genesis, such as the birth of the world and the origin of the human race, remain hotly debated and the "truths" of science are contrasted with the "Truth of Scripture." One needn't be either a scientist or a creationist to be bemused by the contrast of two very different spheres of reality perception. Nor need one be a philosopher or a theologian to profitably read the biblical accounts of creation without worrying too much about how they may contradict the wisdom of Charles Darwin or Stephen Hawking. But it helps to have a teacher and a community to find just how the lessons of Scripture can sit comfortably with those of modern science.

As has always been the case, the best teachers are those who can have conversation with you, for it is in the process of dialogue that knowledge grows. As Jerome puts it, "Spoken words possess an indefinable hidden power, and teaching that passed directly from the mouth of the speaker into the ears of the disciples is more impressive than any other." This is especially true of teaching Scripture, where the truths of one community of readers may not be the same as those of another. To the extent that the Bible reveals the words of God to a community, it is essential that students get those words down right, so that they may become part of the community. In certain communities, once they are part, students of the Bible are free to question, grapple, doubt and deny—so long as they first hear their community's reading of God's word. This is nicely illustrated by the Babylonian Talmud (*Shabbat* 31a) where

> a story is told about a certain gentile who came to Shammai and asked him, "How many Torahs [Bibles] do you Jews have?"
> Shammai responded, "We have two: the written Bible and the Oral Torah which interprets the written one."
> The gentile retorted, "I believe you about the written Bible,

but I have no belief in the oral one. Convert me, but on the condition that you only teach me the written Torah."

Shammai rebuked him and threw him out in disgrace. He came to Hillel where the same conversation took place. Hillel converted him. On the first day Hillel began to teach him Hebrew so that he could read the written Torah. They started with the alphabet. *"Aleph, beth, gimel, daleth,"* Hillel told him, and the proselyte went home repeating the letters in order. The next day he came to Hillel who told him, *"Daleth, gimel, beth, aleph."*

"But," sputtered the proselyte, "yesterday you told them to me the other way around!"

"Well," said Hillel, "you seem dependent upon me to learn how to read Scripture, so perhaps you'll be willing to depend on me for its interpretation as well."

Hillel's wry and crafty lesson to his would-be reader remains valid today. Scripture read plain, like a good novel, is often entertaining, gut-wrenching, even inspirational. But it remains, like a good novel, something that can be read once, then put away and forgotten. It is only in the reading and the rereading which each community does together that the Bible becomes a timeless text, the Word of God. If and when that happens, the Bible ceases to be just another book, gathering dust on a shelf. In a community of readers a conversation takes place. The give and take of interpretation creates an extra voice in the room, the sound of Reading the Book. When that happens, the Bible speaks not only to each community of readers, be they Jewish, Christian or any other flavor, but to all humanity.

How then does a community form which can read and imbue the text with life? Where do we find our Jeromes and Hillels to teach us the rudiments of interpretation? How do we acquire the proper baggage for the journey into Scripture?

Where do we learn the strategies for the battle of bringing the Book alive? And how do we know that we've found the right teacher, the appropriate community, a useful reading strategy? For not all texts are read alike. A recipe is not read the same way that poetry is scanned, even if the line breaks look similar. And the Bible is not the *Odyssey,* even though both are called divine and are frightfully long.

As I suggested above, every act of reading is a journey for which we carry baggage. Put another way, we read through ever-changing lenses, each lens more or less appropriate to the text we read. This baggage or these lenses are a hermeneutic, a means for searching out the meaning of the text before our eyes. Each community carries its own hermeneutic principles about given texts, so that the members of that community know how to read and evaluate those texts. An example is in order here to illustrate my point, for it will also illuminate how various communities approach Scripture.

Picture yourself at the checkout line of the supermarket. As you once again test your patience threshold, you are variously entertained by the tabloid headlines. How do they get away with it? you wonder. My sample headline, which I'm making up just for this occasion: PRINCESS DI DELIVERS TWO-HEADED MONSTER. This is accompanied by a picture of the princess which reminds us why she remains one of the most photographed women in the world.

You do not rush to read the article inside, nor do you immediately buy the tabloid to learn what woe has befallen Princess Di. Perhaps, if the line moves slowly enough, you might peek inside to learn what nonsense is behind the bizarre headline. How do you know to react this way? What hermeneutic principle do you bring to tabloid headlines which makes you doubt the veracity of the sensationalism? What keeps you from credulously repeating with a straight face that Diana had a freak child? It is the community of people who stand on supermarket lines fighting boredom which writes the unwritten rules, the Oral Torah of tabloid headline reading. You just *know* that the headline is misleading, meant to get you to buy the paper, just as you know enough not to pay the fifty or seventy-five cents it might cost you to get the whole scoop on our two-headed monster. You might also realize that somewhere on the supermarket lines, there *are* people whose communal hermeneutic allows this headline to be genuine news. They buy the tabloid; for them it's gospel.

Picture another fictional group of readers, this time on a commuter railroad during the early-morning rush hour. You peek at the *New York Times* over someone's shoulder and read on the book page the following small heading: "Princess Diana Submits Autobiography to Publisher." The subheading goes on: "Diana, Princess of Wales, has delivered a 1,866-page manuscript autobiography consisting of but two chapters. They are provocatively titled 'Lady in Waiting' and 'Princess in Waiting.'"

This latter example, also invented for my point, tells the same story as the tabloid headline: PRINCESS DI DELIVERS TWO-HEADED MONSTER. Now, with certain literary clues, we can decipher the tabloid. "Delivers"—that means submits a manuscript. "Two-Headed"—that means two chapters. "Monster" —that means 1,866 pages. The hermeneutic of railroad commuters reading the *Times* allows us to read this seriously as a news item. It is true. It is "fit to print." In the publishing industry, such an item might be considered Torah. It all depends on where, with whom and how we read. Thanks to Princess Di we can see how the Word is delivered in different ways to different communities of readers with very different impact. The wrong hermeneutic for a text yields the wrong result. The correct interpretation with the correct circumstance gets us closer to the desired facts.

What are the "facts" of my made-up example of Princess Di's book? What questions should be asked? Is the manuscript really that long? Are there only two chapters? Did William Novak really fly to London to ghostwrite this book, too? Will there be photographs? When will the book come out? Or perhaps we should be inquiring about another set of "facts" entirely: Who fathered the monster? Is it humanoid? How did the royal siblings and the Queen react to this delivery? Reading the news is hard work. Learning the facts is a frustrating exercise. Knowing how to value those facts and with whom one may share them more frustrating still. While we're being frustrated, let us remember one more fact about Princess Di's two-headed monster. We can interpret the headlines all we like, but they exist only on the pages of this book. I made them up to illustrate my point. These particular facts are not history, but didactic narrative, created to make a point.

Reading the "facts" of a Book over two thousand years old can be more frustrating still. Even in English translation the Bible seems a foreign tongue. Just as it was for St. Jerome, the style may seem "rude and repellent." How are we to take these stories? Who do we read them with? With whom can we discuss them? How do we approach the Book? Is it to be read as tabloid news, or with all the solemnity of the *Times?* What may we make of its facts? Is it history? Story? What is the point it tries to teach?

Different communities will answer these questions in different ways. Various hermeneutics are employed, even within the same generation, to decipher the meaning of the scriptural text. To a large extent, this is true of reading every text. As the case of Princess Di illustrates, differing hermeneutics dictate not only how the headlines are read and interpreted, but how they are written. In the case of the Bible this is especially so, for by definition (at least within religious communities) the biblical canon is different from any other text. Imbued with the Word of God, the Bible demands a special kind of hermeneutic. True, many of the principles of interpretation are the same as those we use when reading headlines, recipes or poetry. But many ancient interpreters presumed that the Holy Scriptures needed to be read by other rules as well.

Sometimes the biblical text was read as normal human discourse. Sometimes it was read as an elaborate code which needed decipherment. Sometimes each word of Scripture was given its own valence, atomized from the rest of the text and analyzed for meanings not apparent if read in context. Sometimes the text was wholly allegorized, so that each word was taken to mean another thing entirely. Sometimes the text was typologized, so that each word of the Old Testament was taken to refer to the events reported in the New Testament. All in all, over the ages, many different communities adopted many different methods for wrenching meaning out of the biblical text.

To us today these methods seem anachronistic, even violent. They violate what we see as the plain meaning of the scriptural text. We differentiate clearly between the plain meaning (the one we all agree upon) and the other, earlier community's fanciful or forced interpretation. But what is plain to one community may be fanciful to another. What we all agree upon, others may dispute. In short, there is no one common reading of Scripture that everyone can agree with— and there never has been. This is readily apparent when we briefly contemplate how fundamentalist communities read Scripture's message compared with how the same story might be read, say, in a college Western Civilization course.

Even within a given community at a given time there can be more than one reading of Scripture. The Bible's contextual meaning might be profitably contrasted with its religious communal interpretation. For example, the Bible stories told to a Sunday school class may well hew closely to the plot of the narrative. But the same text may be preached from the pulpit with a very different twist for the sake of a moral lesson. The distinction between these two types of reading was recognized many centuries ago by both church and synagogue. The Church Fathers and the Rabbis alike understood that there was more than one way to read Scripture, and that there were many types of profit to be derived from those readings.

The simple meaning, for which the Rabbis employed the Hebrew term *peshat* and which the Church Fathers called the *historic,* is to be distinguished from the homiletical, didactic meaning. These readings of Scripture are on a continuum, however, so that it is often very difficult to discern when simple becomes homiletical. There is a great deal of gray area, where one community's simple may well be another community's homiletical. Despite our inability to always clearly demarcate one reading from another, it is in the homiletical reading that the profoundest hermeneutic hay is made. The homiletical exegesis of Scripture—the "reading out" of moral lessons of the age from the Bible—is what I wish to focus upon in *Reading the Book.*

This type of reading the Book has many different names. The Church Fathers called it homily, or allegory, or commentary. The Rabbis (you'll hear much more about them later) called it searching out, or *midrash*. For them, over a period of more than a thousand years, midrash was *the* means of reading the Book. Through midrashic exegesis moral profit was earned. Through communal reading of Scripture with homiletical commentary and translation, community was formed, reformed and advanced. Midrash was to the Rabbis of old the primary means of hearing God's voice speak through the Word of Scripture.

When we dust the Book off after taking it down from its shelf, we wish to hear it speak. The Bible speaks to us today, as in the past, not by means of a miracle, not by means of audiovisual magic, but by communal effort. We struggle to make sense of a text that has spoken to our ancestors now for two millennia and more. It has inspired poets, novelists, prophets and mystics. When we read the Bible and search its words for meaning today, we do midrash. Through midrash we are linked to the exegetical activities of the Rabbis of old, to the Fathers and Doctors of the Church, to the poets and writers of every generation. This type of hermeneutic, this ability to open the biblical text to new meaning, allows us to open ourselves to the possibility of finding meaning. We can connect to the past, we can connect to the community with whom we read and share our dialogue with Scripture. Midrash lets us search for ourselves.

Reading the Book is about midrashic readings of Scripture. It is an attempt to open the biblical text to modern interpretation by exposition of an age-old method of reading. Midrashic method is found within the Bible itself. When, in Genesis, the names of the patriarchs are explicated by folk etymologies, it is midrash. Sometimes it isn't even very good midrash. The Bible comments in Genesis 5:29, "So he called his name Noah, saying, 'This one will comfort us' [Hebrew:

yenahamenu]." The apparent explanation of Noah's name is based on a bad pun, Noah for *yenahamenu*. The Rabbis comment: The name is not the midrash, nor the midrash the name. That is to say, the Bible's interpretation of the name Noah as "comfort" is a bad interpretation, for "Noah" and "comfort" do not, in fact, share the same Hebrew root. The Rabbis like a good pun as well as the next guy, but not a poorly wrought pun. Still, the Rabbis recognize explicitly here that the Bible is doing midrash on Noah's name.

Midrashic process continues throughout the Bible. Deuteronomy could be considered a midrash on the first four books of the Torah. Consider, if you will, the way Deuteronomy 9 whitewashes the role of Aaron in the incident of the Golden Calf, as opposed to the version of the story in Exodus 32 in which Aaron is an active participant. The works of the prophets also are in some way midrash on the Torah, while the latter Writings are midrashic expansions of earlier works —look at the relationship of Chronicles to the books of Samuel and Kings.

The earliest translation of Scripture, the Septuagint translation of the Torah into Greek, is also a kind of midrash, since all translation perforce interprets. Later expansions of the canonical works of the Bible may also be considered midrashic in style. And certain passages of the New Testament may be considered to have performed some sort of midrashic process on the Old Testament passages they ponder and rework.

When the Jerusalem Temple was destroyed by the Romans in the year 70 C.E.,* the job of midrash began in earnest. The sacrificial cult of the Bible came to an end, and it fell to the Rabbis to interpret and reinterpret Scripture so that Judaism

* Common Era, which is used instead of the Christian designation A.D. Similarly, B.C.E., Before the Common Era, is used instead of B.C.

might continue apace, both through its behavioral-legal mechanics and its spiritual life.

This continuity of process, the ongoing interpretation that the Rabbis inherited, makes them candidates for a careful study of Reading the Book. From 70 C.E. to about 1000, the rabbinic communities of the Land of Israel, Babylonia and, later, Europe engaged in midrashic reading of Scripture. Their strategies kept the text timeless, alive and meaningful for each and every generation. Earlier comments were passed on, modified, retold, so that the Bible became a patchwork quilt of text, with a verse of Scripture at the center and the various interpretations of the verse radiating outward to form the fabric. This quilt of scriptural interpretation offered warmth to all who sheltered under it. Like a family quilt, it was simultaneously an heirloom, linking the user to all previous generations, and a functional cover, expanding as new patches were sewn onto the already extant woof and warp.

I have chosen to focus on midrash as a means of reading the Book because of its ongoing tradition of interpretation. I use it as my paradigm for communal reading of Scripture because the method held sway within Jewish communities for almost 930 years (the length of days of biblical Adam) and then was faithfully transmitted along with other methods of interpretation for as many years again, up to the modern era. Along with the comments and methods of the Rabbis, I will consider the various readings of Scripture offered by the Church Fathers. Where it helps, I will compare and contrast their comments, but in the main, the methods of the Fathers of the church and synagogue are similar.

I emphasize the Rabbis here not only because of their unbroken tradition of reading the Book, but also, not coincidentally, because I, too, am a rabbi. I study midrash for a living;

my religious bias lies with my ancestors. If I prefer their method of reading the Book, it is because it is mine. When I turn to the Church Fathers for insight, it is because there is profit to be found there as well. Reading the Book demands that we listen to good exegesis no matter who offers it. While it is a communal process, it cannot be done exclusively within the confines of any one community. A true exegete who seeks to hear the word of God in Scripture must explore every avenue of interpretation. If, when it has been explored, it fits within the parameters of the community, good. If not, insight has been gained into the interpretative traditions of our neighbors. We read the same Book, differently. We seek to hear the same Voice, differently. An early midrash on the Book of Exodus, commenting on the revelation at Mount Sinai, suggests that when God's voice was heard by the six hundred thousand Israelites, each person heard God differently, in a voice appropriate to that person's needs.

For the interpretation of Scripture to be revelatory, we must reveal ourselves, too. As the *Midrash to Proverbs* puts it, commenting on Proverbs 31:14, " 'She is like a merchant ship, gathering bread from afar'—if a person does not reveal himself when learning Scripture, he will never learn it." We must gather from afar as well as near so that our reading of the Book is truly beneficial. So though my concentration will be on my own religious tradition of midrashic interpretation, I will turn to the Fathers of the Church, as I have already, for their insights and wisdom. It is likewise my hope that Christians and other non-Jewish readers will gather wisdom from the Rabbis so that their own reading of Scripture will be continually beneficial.

Who are these Rabbis? When did they live? What is this Midrash they preached and wrote? These and other questions are necessary for us to get on with the enterprise of learning how the rabbinic community engaged in midrash. A brief rather than long answer to these questions will be offered here. We are blessed now, in the late twentieth century, with a wealth of books in English about the Rabbis, their culture and their literature. Though most of those books are written for Jewish audiences, many are accessible to any interested reader.

The veil of mystery about ancient Judaism has slowly vanished, and the Rabbis have emerged as wise and witty readers of the Bible. Their canny interpretations created a vibrant Judaism that flourished alongside a burgeoning Christianity in the Roman Empire. The Rabbis who will be quoted in this book, along with their Church contemporaries, flourished in the era called late antiquity, from approximately the first through the sixth centuries of the Common Era. I will, on occasion, quote rabbis from as late as the eleventh century (for me, practically the modern era), and will cite texts compiled even later. Since the works in which rabbinic comments are collected inevitably date from well after the time in which individual rabbis lived, we can never be sure that a statement attributed to a rabbi actually was said by him or even reliably dates from that era. Still, unless there seems to be good reason to doubt an attribution of a statement to a given rabbi, we will accept it as from his era. As we saw with Princess Di's two-headed monster, the facts of a story need not have happened, they can be attributed to a historic personality for the sake of teaching a lesson. Since midrashic literature is, above all, interested in lesson teaching, we must keep the rabbinic propensity for blurring story and history in clear sight.

The Rabbis called their interpretations of Scripture, legends, stories and laws the Oral Torah. As we learned from the story of Hillel and Shammai, the Rabbis thought of two parallel Torahs: the written Bible and their own readings of it. In the period of the Rabbis, their Oral Torah was, indeed, very much oral. Along with their Palestinian contemporary, Jerome, they put great faith in the power of spoken teaching. The Rabbis, though often quite literate in other areas, chose to transmit their teachings verbally. And although substantial portions of the rabbinic community were fluent in Greek as well as their own communal Hebrew and Aramaic, they chose to transmit their Oral Torah primarily in Hebrew with some portions of the literature in Aramaic. This, of course, distinguishes rabbinic midrash from the interpretative works of the Church Fathers, transmitted to us in Greek, Latin and Syriac.

The Church Fathers were also concerned with composing literature. Even their extemporaneous sermons were copied by shorthand experts and edited and revised for written circulation. Not so the Rabbis. Their early sermons were delivered on the Sabbath, when it was prohibited to write. No doubt, disciples made a fair effort to memorize the sermons, interpretations and homilies of their masters, but their oral literature often suffers from inaccuracy in transmission.

On occasion, rabbinic works were designed for ease of oral transmission, with mnemonic devices to aid the reciters. These works were behavioral-legal, the prime example being the earliest redacted document of Oral Torah, the Mishnah. Edited around the year 200 C.E. by the patriarch of the Palestinian Jewish community, the Mishnah enjoyed immediate prestige. It was recited and commented upon in rabbinic academies in both the Land of Israel and Babylonia, and was the basis for the two later major corpora, the Babylonian and Palestinian Talmuds.

The Mishnah is not only important as an oral document that embodies the earliest rabbinic teachings, it is important in form as well. Unlike most other rabbinic documents, the Mishnah and its two Talmuds are *not* structured as Bible commentary. Rather, the Mishnah is divided into six anthropological categories or orders: Agriculture, Calendar, Matters Pertaining to Women, Torts, Sacred Items and Taboos. Each order of the Mishnah is then subdivided into tractates, so Calendar has subcategories such as Sabbath and Yom Kippur. Yet, even within this structure, the Rabbis remain so bibliocentric that the Mishnah is dotted with scriptural commentaries and the later Talmuds are awash with them. In the pages of this book you will find comments from the Mishnah (Palestine, ca. 200 C.E.), the Palestinian Talmud (ca. 425 C.E.) and the Babylonian Talmud (ca. 475 C.E.).

For all that the pronouncements of the Mishnah held a central place in the loose canon of Oral Torah, exegetical midrash abounded. Since it was relatively easy to collect midrashim in the order of the scriptural verses they comment on, later written collections of earlier oral commentaries and homilies are found in great number. Again, these are in the main in Hebrew, with scattered portions in Aramaic. Most of these collections are Palestinian, a few are European or Babylonian. One can find midrash collections on virtually every book of the Hebrew Bible. Sometimes more than one collection exists for a given book, particularly the books of the Pentateuch, a portion of which was read in synagogue every Sabbath. Often, when a section of the Torah is legalistic, it attracted legal commentary, or *halachic* midrash. Where the material is moral-didactic or narrative, the commentary is a looser social-ethical type of midrash called *aggadic*. *Aggada* simply means storytelling, and one medieval rabbi defined

Aggada as everything that is not Halacha (law). As you can imagine, aggadic midrash casts a very wide net, and many, many volumes abound. As I've said, the point of reading the Book with the tools of aggadic midrash was to hear God's voice in the words of Scripture; or as the Midrash (*Sifre Deuteronomy*) itself tells it: "Do you wish to know The-One-Who-Spoke-And-So-The-World-Was? Learn Aggada, for it is there that God's ways are explicated."

Here I should explicate some of the ways that midrash operates on Scripture to yield exegesis. I wish only to offer some very broad characteristics, since the remainder of this book will serve up abundant examples of the various methods. In the main it helps to understand that there are two overall worldviews when approaching midrashic exegesis of Scripture, which are most often represented by the so-called schools of two great second-century Rabbis, Aqiba and Ishmael. For Rabbi Ishmael, "the Torah speaks in human discourse"—that is, Scripture is subject to the same redundancies and occasional verbiage that we all encounter in desultory conversation. Rabbi Aqiba is represented as adamantly opposed to Ishmael's point of view. If Scripture is the Word of God, then no word is superfluous. Every repetition and redundancy bears special meaning. This view is carried so far, in later midrash, that individual letters and even parts of letters are subject to exegesis!

The Aqiban view, by the way, is shared by many of the Church Fathers. The great third-century Bible scholar Origen of Caesarea, a Palestinian who lived a century after Aqiba, says:

I suppose every letter, no matter how strange, which is written in the oracle of God, does its work. And there is not one jot or tittle written in the Scripture, which, when men know how to extract the virtue, does not work its own work. . . .

The saint is a sort of spiritual herbalist who culls from the sacred Scripture every jot and every common letter, discovers the value of what is written and its use, and finds there is nothing in the Scripture superfluous.

Our friend St. Jerome also jumps on the Aqiban bandwagon, as it were, when he writes (in a commentary on the New Testament Epistle to the Ephesians), "In the divine Scriptures every word, syllable, accent and point is packed with meaning."

For the Rabbis and Church Fathers, then, reading the Book was an adventure, a journey to a grand palace with many great and awesome halls, banquet rooms and chambers, as well as many passages and locked doors. The adventure lay in learning the secrets of the palace, unlocking all the doors and perhaps catching a glimpse of the King in all His splendor. As Origen put it, crediting his Jewish Hebrew teacher with whom he often discussed the meaning of biblical passages:

That great scholar used to say that inspired Scripture taken as a whole was . . . like many locked-up rooms in one house. Before each room he supposed a key to be placed, but not the one belonging to it; and that the keys were so dispersed all round the rooms. . . . It would be a troublesome piece of work to discover the keys to suit the rooms they were meant for. It was, he said, just so with the understanding of the Scriptures. . . . The only way to begin to understand them was by means of other passages.

Origen's insight merits some comment. The earliest form of scriptural interpretation was explicating Scripture by means of other verses of Scripture. This served a dual purpose. It not only unlocked difficult verses, it also promoted the notion that the biblical canon, made up of disparate books written in different countries over the course of centuries, was the one, unified Word of God. This method of using one verse to explain another is found as early as the Passover Haggadah, a document used by families in their evening celebration of the Passover seder, and originating shortly after the destruction of the Jerusalem Temple in the first century of the Common Era.

Contemporary with this type of exegesis, the first-century sectarians who lived on the shores of the Dead Sea at Qumran used simple equations to unravel their Scripture. After a biblical verse the Dead Sea scrolls often comment, "That means . . ." and an allegorical apocalyptic interpretation referring to their own community follows. The equation of a verse or a part of a verse with another verse or an allegorical reading is the simplest, most direct form of midrash. It is a form of exegesis we have already encountered in our attempt to explain and reconcile the tabloid headline invented above, with the *Times* headline invented for the same occasion: "Delivers—that means submits a manuscript. Two-Headed—that means two chapters. Monster—that means 1,866 pages."

Our return to Princess Di offers a good opportunity to take a breath and see where this book is going. Now that you've been briefly introduced to the Rabbis of the Midrash, I'd like to take the next couple of chapters to tell you more about their hermeneutic. First we'll see how they viewed the Bible; we'll learn that they were careful and critical readers of Scripture, not cable television fundamentalists. Once we learn how they view the written Torah, we'll take a look at how they see the Oral Torah as an ongoing continuation of the revelation at Sinai.

With the groundwork laid, we can begin our journey into Scripture, particularly how the Rabbis read the Book. We'll study their strategies beginning with the Abraham narratives from the Book of Genesis, and then peruse rabbinic versions of the biblical narratives about the men and women who people the Pentateuch. At that point, we can get back to basics and read how the Rabbis and their contemporaries understood the creation of humanity. Finally, we can jump back even further in time to the creation of the universe and learn the importance of reading the Book for the architecture of the universe.

Chapter Two

GOD DICTATES,
MOSES COMPOSES

The Rabbis were not fundamentalists—they didn't even watch cable television. This is about the only sure generalization we can make about so broad a grouping of individuals, who lived during the four-hundred-year period from the late first through the fifth centuries of the Common Era. The literatures that preserve their writings span an even longer period, more than a millennium, and comprise such a vast array of books and opinions that one large segment is referred to as the Sea of the Talmud. Like the ocean, various and contradictory forms of life may be found there, so one works very hard to avoid absolutes such as "the Rabbis never" or "the Rabbis always."

This having been said, I will repeat my assertion above, knowing that one can search rabbinic literature and find a refutation of what I suggest. Nevertheless, let me offer my thesis and evidence to buttress it: The Rabbis were not fundamentalists. In order to say this, it is necessary for me to describe what I think a fundamentalist is, so it will be perfectly clear what the Rabbis are not.

A fundamentalist, when it comes to biblical matters, believes that the entire Bible is *literally* the word of God. This position carries with it a variety of corollaries, each of which amplifies the essential fundamentalist myth. If the Bible is literally, entirely the word of God, it was spoken on one occasion. The position of the fundamentalists demands that the word of God be revealed all at once at one time, yet paradoxically be apposite for all occasions, no matter when.

This eternal aspect of the one-fell-swoop revelation is itself confirmed by a second corollary to the fundamentalist stance. If the Bible is literally in its entirety the word of God, it is a unified document, without contradiction or error. The fundamentalist will tell you the Bible is inerrant, it cannot be wrong, no matter what we moderns may think. The fundamentalist will insist on the inerrancy of the Bible despite the discoveries of historians, archeologists, geologists, physicists, biologists and the like. For the fundamentalists, scientists like Charles Darwin and Stephen Hawking are not great thinkers, they are misguided heretics.

The greatest fount of critical inquiry in the rabbinic world in this century is a collection of more than one hundred thousand ancient manuscripts and fragments of texts dating from the ninth to the eighteenth century which can be used to test and challenge the readings of traditional Jewish texts. This collection, found in the late nineteenth century in an antechamber of the synagogue in Fustat, Egypt, and referred to today as the Cairo Geniza documents, is housed in the Rare Book and Manuscript Collection of the University Library in Cambridge, England. (It is no small satisfaction that this mass of critical texts is housed in the library of Dr. Hawking's university, stored next to the diaries of another scholar late of Cambridge, Charles Darwin.)

Fundamentalists are threatened by the kinds of critical thinking these men and manuscripts represent. They do not like their firmly held opinions challenged by knowledge or facts or variant readings. They do not like natural selection or the big-bang theory. They prefer opinion over knowledge. Ask them; they will confirm their opinion by faith. It need not be proven by reason, or verified through evidence. It is Truth. It comes from the Bible, inerrant, the word of God. So, the fundamentalists.

This is true of all the fundamentalists, be they Christians or Jews. But Jewish and Christian fundamentalists do differ radically on what they consider to be the Bible. Jews, whether fundamentalists or critical thinkers, have a different Bible than do Christians. First and foremost, Jews do not have a New Testament. None of the gospels, acts or epistles are part of the Jewish Bible. Indeed, the Jews don't even have an Old Testament. For Jews, there is but one Bible, the one they have seemingly always had, never superseded or even joined by a New Testament. By definition, theirs is not the Old Testament, it is simply the Bible.

In fact, it's not even really that. For Jews, it is the *Tanakh,* a name that is a Hebrew acronym for the constituent parts of the Hebrew Bible. *Ta* for Torah—the Pentateuch or Five Books of Moses (Genesis, Exodus, Leviticus, Numbers and Deuteronomy). *Na* for Neviim or Prophets—the second section of the Bible, which includes the historical works of Joshua, Judges, Samuel and Kings, as well as the prophetic works of Isaiah, Jeremiah and Ezekiel along with the Twelve: Hosea, Joel, Amos, Obadiah, Jonah, Micah, Nahum, Habakkuk, Zephaniah, Haggai, Zachariah and Malachi. (I confess I had to go look up the list of these twelve so-called Minor Prophets. I once tried to memorize the list when I used to commute an hour to teach a Bible class, but every time I tried to recite the list I shut my eyes to concentrate on getting the order right. Since I was the driver, my fellow teacher convinced me that I was better off looking up the names rather than getting us both killed trying to memorize them.)

The last part of the acronym Tanakh is for Ketuvim—Hagiographa or Writings. This motley collection includes the Psalms, Proverbs, Job, the Five Scrolls (Song of Songs, Ruth, Lamentations, Ecclesiastes, Esther), Daniel, Ezra-Nehemiah (counted as one book) and Chronicles (also counted as one book, though divided into two parts, just like the prophetic works of Samuel and Kings).

Those of you with Christian versions of Scripture will recognize not only that the New Testament is absent, but that the order of the books differs. There is one further difference, but it cuts in part across churches, too. The Hebrew Bible does not include the books of the Apocrypha as part of the canon. Works like the Wisdom of Solomon or Ben Sirach, histories like Maccabees, the stories of Judith, Tobit and certain additions to the Hebrew text are simply absent, as in Daniel and Esther. So the Hebrew Bible (an awkward rendering of Tanakh and, as writer/editor David Rosenberg once quipped, about as meaningless to Jews as the phrase English Shakespeare) differs in language, order and content from the Church's Old Testament.

But, whatever shape the canon of their Bible may take, be they Jew or Christian, Protestant or Roman Catholic, fundamentalists resent critical analysis of the Bible. If the Bible is the word of God, they ask, how can it be subject to criticism? Further, if it is subject to criticism, if it is treated as we would treat any other book, where then lies the source of religious authority? If the Bible is but the words of humans, why trust it? How can a human document serve as the source of religious authority?

Given the general modes of critical analysis of Scripture, these are fair, even intelligent, questions. We'll see how the Rabbis dealt with the problem of authority in the next chapter. Here, however, I'd like to focus on other questions: Were the Rabbis critical readers of the Bible? Could they discern the textual problems inherent in modern readings of Scripture and still be the proponents of faith they are correctly thought to be? Did they read the Bible that closely? Did they not, in fact, think that the Bible was literally the word of God? If not, what did the Rabbis think about the Bible? Further, what did the Rabbis understand when they heard and used the phrase "word of God"?

Let us begin with examining the rabbinic opinion about what I characterized above as the fundamentalist myth—that the entire Bible is literally the word of God. This assumes that all three parts of the Jewish Bible—Torah (Pentateuch), Neviim (Prophets) and Ketuvim (Hagiographa), that is to say the entire Tanakh—should be understood as literally the word of God. Further, the myth presumes that this unified divine Scripture provides the correct answer for every issue without brooking contradiction.

To test this myth, let me start with what seems to be a safe bet. The Bible has a uniform stance toward sin, right? Well, it's not so easy. First, sin is defined in a broad variety of ways throughout the Bible. But even assuming that there was one notion of sin, there is more than one antidote offered to cure it. The Book of Leviticus prescribes, ad nauseum, that animal sacrifice is the correct atonement for sin. Blood on the altar is thought to be an efficacious means of averting God's wrath, of cleansing the impurities from the congregation. But the prophets capture the message differently. They suggest that God admonishes the Israelites: "It is love I want, not blood sacrifice!"

This contradiction about how to expiate as basic a biblical category as sin points to the problem of history—all of the Bible did not stem from one era. Following the destruction of the First Temple in 587 B.C.E., when the Jews went into exile and could no longer offer sacrifice, it made sense for the prophets to downplay the importance of the sacrificial cult and offer in its stead a means of atonement available to all. In other words, the divine Word may be time-bound. God may speak to particular situations of history.

My teacher, Father Raymond E. Brown, pointed out a beautiful example of this phenomenon. Everybody knows (and quotes) the stirring words of Isaiah (2:4): "Beat your swords into plowshares, your spears into pruning-hooks." But very few people know (and almost no one, including the Rabbis, quotes) the prophet Joel (4:10, 3:10 RSV), who exhorts, "Beat your plowshares into swords, your pruning-hooks into spears." Hard to beat this for a contradiction within Scripture! But the point above applies here, too. God's word was apparently bound to given events of history. When war was called for, God spoke through Joel to rouse the people to fight. When peace was needed, God spoke through Isaiah to preach nonviolence. That one prophet apparently knew and played with the words of the other was all the more delightful—it made clear the urgency of God's message. There are occasions when God's word seems to be stood on its head; we've just seen the Bible itself attest to it.

It is one thing to say that the contradictions within Scripture can be harmonized. The standard method of the Rabbis when confronting such contradictions is to attribute them to differing eras. The Rabbis do not share the fundamentalist view that God's word was spoken but once, for all time. They seem to say, as do the modern Bible critics, that the text unfolded over the course of a very long time. Does this mean that the Rabbis deny the rest of the fundamentalist myth? Perhaps they would agree that the entire Bible is literally the word of God, even though it is time-bound. Perhaps not. In fact, the Rabbis openly express their doubt that the entire Bible is the word of God.

The Babylonian sage Rav Yehuda quotes his master, Samuel (*Megillah 7a*), who asserts that the scroll of Esther is lacking divine inspiration entirely. To quote more precisely, "It was not spoken by [the inspiration of] the holy spirit." Now Samuel surely noticed that the Hebrew Book of Esther neglects to mention God anywhere among its verses (just as did the Greek translator, who bent over backward to reinsert You-Know-Who into the text), so perhaps Samuel thought that if God was not mentioned by name, God's authorship (or better, authority) was doubtful. Or perhaps Samuel felt that the book was a romantic farce, a comedy better left to the drunken revels of the holiday of Purim on which it was read in the synagogues. If so, Samuel had a profound understanding of the Book of Esther, but nowhere does he tell us this is his reason for being so dubious. Maybe he took a literary bent and descried the lack of Omniscient Narrator in the novel called Esther (this problem is actually alluded to in the talmudic discussion of Esther). Whatever his reasons, Samuel denies the divine voice in Esther and so breaks the myth of a unified Scripture entirely and literally the word of God.

But this is not all, not by any means. Rabbi Meir, a second-century sage, who earned his living as a scribe, expressed
his doubts about other books of Scripture which he copied.
Before I lay out Rabbi Meir's worries, let me share a story
about him which exemplifies the seriousness with which he
took his work as a copyist of sacred texts. It is said that Rabbi
Meir was once visiting Asia Minor just before the holiday of
Purim, when the scroll of Esther is read. The synagogue of
the locale did not own a scroll and wished to commission
Rabbi Meir to produce one for them in time for the holiday.
Yet Meir knew that Jewish law prohibits ritual use of a scroll
copied from memory. The Rabbis frowned on using such a
scroll in the synagogue since one could not necessarily trust
the memory of any scribe, even a Rabbi Meir. So rabbinic
law provided that for a scroll to be "kosher" for synagogue
use, it had to be copied from another scroll. Meir, stranded in
Asia Minor, displayed his cleverness (and literalness) and
solved the problem for the community. First, he copied a
scroll out from memory. This scroll could not be used for the
reading in the synagogue on Purim. But then Meir copied
that scroll and so used the second in compliance with the
dictates of rabbinic law!

In any case, on another occasion Rabbi Meir suggested that
the Book of Ecclesiastes did not belong in the canon. A generation later, Rabbi Shimon ben Menasiah explained that the
book was not divine, it was but the (cynical) wisdom of
Solomon. In other words, there were Rabbis who felt that
Ecclesiastes was but a human product.

Rabbi Meir pointed out further that there was a good deal
of disagreement in the rabbinic community over the status of
the Song of Songs. The book was redeemed for the canon by

reading it allegorically as the story of God's love for Israel (or, in Christian circles, as Christ's love for the Church). Indeed, the powerful and prominent Rabbi Aqiba insisted that all songs are holy, and the Song of Songs is the Holy of Holies. Still, Meir was honest enough to admit that not all of the Rabbis shared Aqiba's opinion. There were those who could not disguise the fact that what they were reading was erotic poetry. As the modern translator of Song of Songs, H. L. Ginsberg, says in his preface to the New Jewish Version, "The book is entirely profane." According to Rabbi Meir, there were Rabbis of old who might have agreed with this assessment.

One final example of how the Rabbis openly doubted that the entire Bible was the word of God comes from the Book of Job. Some Rabbis suggest that Job never existed, or in their own quaint phrasing, "He didn't exist and weren't created." Perhaps they make Job into a character of fiction because Job 14:14 ("If a man dies, will he live again?") seems to deny afterlife, otherwise a tenet of rabbinic theology. Perhaps the Rabbis just could not bear that a gentile should garner so much of God's attention. Whatever the case may be, even those who championed Job were unclear exactly when he lived. Those who held the work a fiction could hardly be said to be firm supporters of the divine authorship of the book.

These few examples suffice to show us that the Rabbis were not fundamentalists, and that some Rabbis openly doubted the divine authorship of many books of Scripture. Perhaps if we narrow our focus, we will find that the Rabbis thought the Torah was given by God to Moses at Sinai. This is a phrase which is found in rabbinic literature and which will be defined in detail in the next chapter. For now, we ask the fundamentalist question—did the Rabbis believe that the whole Torah, the Pentateuch or Five Books of Moses, was given in its entirety at one moment (more precisely forty days) at Sinai?

This fundamentalist view would reject implicitly any notion of modern critical study of the Bible and almost all Bible scholars in this century accept some version of the notion that the Pentateuch is made up of various sources. These sources were edited or redacted together, say the critics, well after the time of Moses, most likely during the exilic period following the destruction of the first Jerusalem Temple in 587 B.C.E. The critics discern four major sources that make up the Torah, which they often designate by the initials J, E, D and P. P refers to the Priestly source, which has fragments scattered through the Pentateuch but most clearly shows its hand in the authorship of the Book of Leviticus (the Priestly book). D refers to the Deuteronomist.

J and E are a bit more difficult, but are generally taken to refer to the two narrative strands, most visible in Genesis and early Exodus, that use distinctive epithets for God. E refers to those verses of Scripture that refer to God as Elohim, which means judge but which is also the Hebrew name for God. J refers to those strands of narrative that employ the tetragrammaton, God's personal name, which was spelled out by German scholars as Jahweh (often incorrectly rendered into English as Jehovah), hence J. A quick set of examples is in order here to illustrate why critics think the biblical narrative is made up of varying strands.

Let's begin with a pop quiz. How was Eve created? Most of you will answer, from Adam's rib, and that is correct, it says so in Genesis 2:21. But some of you may equally correctly cite Genesis 1:27: "Elohim created the earthperson [to borrow Phyllis Trible's felicitous translation] in God's image, in the image of Elohim God created it, male and female God created them." Here, man and woman are created simultaneously, together, equally in God's image. Later in this book we will see how the Rabbis harmonized these two stories, but for now suffice it to say that the Rabbis also recognized the possibility of two varying stories, and, perhaps, two varying sources.

A second quiz question: Who was Joseph sold to? Think hard now—was it the Midianites or the Ishmaelites? Genesis 37:28 tells us that Midianite merchants drew Joseph out of the pit where his brothers had left him. The remainder of the verse reports that they sold him to Ishmaelites who brought him down to Egypt. So far so good? Read on, for Genesis 37:36 reports, "The Midianites sold Joseph to Egypt." Can the story be harmonized? Yes. Must it be? Not if you agree with the critics and assume that two versions of the story (J and E) were woven here into one tapestry of narrative.

If all of this alphabet soup of criticism is disturbing, if you are unhappy to learn that today's scholars make the Bible into a loom work of interwoven sources, know that you are not alone. Most readers are distressed to hear how thoroughly critics and other close readers of the Bible have unraveled the fundamentalist myth. I recall having lectured on this topic in a synagogue in Washington, D.C., in the late 1970s. When I got to this point in my lecture, a gentleman began shaking his head negatively and brandishing his Bible at me, as though it could ward off the vampire effect of my remarks. I sought to assuage his discomfort by offering an analogy which I thought appropriate to the nation's capital.

"You in Washington know things that we in the rest of

America can only guess at," I began. "When President Carter gives a speech, I hear it on television and it sounds coherent. Yet you here know that a presidential speech is made up of many parts. Different speechwriters contribute differing segments. Differing cabinet members and security council members seek to have their views heard. Different congressional members wish to have their opinions aired through the presidential voice. The president finally makes his own decisions, sifts through the various drafts and opinions and then goes on television to deliver policy."

My audience chuckled appreciatively at my analogy and I concluded my lecture. All the same, I kept a wary eye out for my book waver, since he didn't seem thoroughly placated by my explanation. During the refreshment hour immediately following the services, my would-be interlocutor came straight for me. "You know," he opened without any introduction, "if the Bible was composed the way speeches are written here in Washington, we're in far, far worse shape than I imagined."

Now it was my turn to chuckle appreciatively. The man turned to leave and then stopped. "You don't know who I am, do you?" I confessed that he had me at a disadvantage. He smiled broadly and stuck out a hand. "I'm Stuart Eizenstat," he said, "President Carter's domestic affairs adviser."

The folks in Washington were not the only ones to be disturbed by the nuances of text; the Rabbis of old separated J from E as well. Though they recognized the problem of the differing names for God which crisscross the Genesis narrative, they solved the problem in a different way than the modern critics do. E was Elohim, Hebrew for judge. So, the Rabbis homilized, whenever the text refers to God as Elohim, it refers to God's attribute of strict justice. J was the tetra-grammaton, the private, personal name for God. When the J word is employed, it refers to God's attribute of mercy. Through this creative homily the Rabbis not only explain away two variant uses of God's name from two discernible strands of narrative, they put the narrative into perspective. J and E are in dynamic tension with one another. Our being judged as humans, as God's creatures, depends on the balance found between God's strict justice and God's mercy. The Rabbis understood how to turn a critical insight into a didactic lesson without falling prey to fundamentalism.

But what did the Rabbis actually think about God's giving the Torah at Sinai? Which was it—God dictates or Moses composes? There is a passage in the Talmud (*Gittin 60a*) that discusses two points of view on what happened at Sinai. It is shaped, like most Talmudic passages, as a disagreement. It looks, at first blush, like a disagreement between the fundamentalists and the critics whom I have been describing above. But before pigeonholing the points of view in the text, let's give it a careful reading.

"Some say the Torah was given scroll by scroll." This opinion seems to suggest that the Pentateuch was revealed one section at a time. The eleventh-century French rabbinic exegete, Rashi, whose commentary has accompanied every printed edition of the Talmud, explains: "When a section was spoken [by God] to Moses, he wrote it down. After forty years, Moses stitched them all together." Rashi's explanation leaves this Talmudic opinion sounding all the more like the modern source critics. Rashi suggests that Moses literally acts as the redactor, sewing together the various sections until he has one pentateuchal text, even if its seams did show.

READING THE BOOK..................... 34

But what of the other Talmudic opinion, the one I alluded
to above, which might support the fundamentalist viewpoint?
The Talmud teaches, "Some say the Torah was given sealed."
Is this, then, the fundamentalist view and the refutation of my
thesis stated at the beginning of the chapter? (I did warn you
that the refutation could be found in the literature.) Let us see
what Rashi has to say about this passage: "Moses memorized
all that God said to him and at the end of forty years wrote it
all down." Rashi's reading of this text is far from the fundamentalist myth. In fact, it is outrageous—for as my colleague
David Kraemer once pointed out, Rashi seems to be saying
that even the written Torah is Oral Torah!

Moses relies on a very human memory, the memory of a
man from age eighty to one hundred twenty, to keep the
revelation straight in his head. After a forty-year period of
keeping the revelation in his memory, presumably reciting
and editing along the way, only then does Moses redact his
sources into the Five Books that bear his name. What did he
forget during those years? What did he omit? What might he
have added on his own to make the text more understandable,
even more palatable or appropriate to the ever-changing conditions of desert life?

Both Talmudic opinions demand a more nuanced view of
revelation than the extremes we have been positing for the
sake of our argument. The word of God, according to the
Talmud, involves human participation. Either the Word is
redacted by a human editor or transmitted by a human memory. Either way, humanity is involved in the reception and
transmission of the word of God. The Rabbis were not fundamentalists—the entire Bible was not literally in its entirety
the word of God, given at one moment and inerrant. To the

extent that humanity was the hearer of the Word and to the extent that humans transmitted the Word, mistakes could creep in, contradictions crop up, editing take place. The Rabbis of old were not quite twentieth-century critics, but they weren't fundamentalists.

But maybe if we just narrow the scope of the myth once more, we'll find the Rabbis in concurrence. Surely even the Rabbis would agree that God gave the Ten Commandments on Mount Sinai. After all, they saw the movie, it has to be true. Well, they *didn't* see the movie, so they don't quite have the gospel of Cecil B. DeMille to rely on. In fact, a medieval story tells how the Rabbis imagined God worrying about the problem of imputed authorship of the Ten Commandments:

> When the Holy, praised be He, desired to give the Ten Commandments, Moses stood at God's side. God said to him, "I intend to roll back the heavens and say, 'I am the Lord your God' (Exodus 20:2) and they'll say, 'Who said that, the Holy, praised be He, or Moses?' So Moses, go down the mountain and then I'll say, 'I am the Lord your God.' "
>
> Thus the Holy, praised be He, said to Moses (Exodus 19:10), "Go down to the people and sanctify them today and tomorrow. . . ." While Moses was descending God was revealed, as it is said, "And Moses descended to the people" (Exodus 19:25), and immediately following (Exodus 20:1), "And then God spoke all these words, saying, 'I am the Lord your God. . . .' "

This humorous midrash explains some of the difficult choreography in Exodus chapters 19 and 20, which report the events before and during the giving of the Ten Commandments. But they also reveal, along the way, the rabbinic awareness that not everybody would attribute the Ten Commandments directly to God. Rather, there would be those who suggest that Moses had some hand even in the authorship of the Ten Commandments. This feeling, that it was a human, not God, who authored even the Ten Commandments, finds its basis in Scripture.

The first two of the Ten Commandments (according to the Jewish reckoning which counts the verse "I am the Lord your God [Exodus 20:2] as number 1) are written in the first person. God says, "I am," and "have no other gods before Me," and "I am a jealous God." But the remaining eight commandments are second-person commands, with no whiff of the "I am." So the Talmud suggests (*Makkot 24a*) that God spoke only the first two commandments. When the people grew terrified they asked Moses to intercede. It was Moses who spoke the rest.

There are, then, Rabbis who think that only the first two of the Ten Commandments are the word of God. This hardly qualifies for the fundamentalist myth set out above, that the entire Bible is literally God's word. As if this weren't enough, the extent of God's involvement in revelation finds even greater limitation in rabbinic literature. The great scholar of Jewish mysticism, Gershom Scholem, tells the story of a nineteenth-century Chassidic master, Menahem Mendel of the town of Rymanov, who once suggested that only the first letter of the Ten Commandments was spoken by God. Moses then interceded, as suggested above, and it was the human intermediary who spoke the rest.

For Rabbi Mendel this allows the Bible to be a mystical document which, humanly mediated, is wholly subject to human (and mystical) interpretation. Mendel's reading of Scripture is not without its humorous irony. He limits God's participation to the pronounciation of but one letter. Yet, the first letter of the Ten Commandments is the letter *aleph,* an unvoiced consonant. Without a vowel to help this letter along, no sound is made when an *aleph* is found in a word. So when the people at Sinai heard God pronounce *aleph,* they did not wish to take their chances at hearing God pronounce a voiced letter. It was then, in fear, that they asked Moses to intercede. According to Rabbi Mendel, God's "Word" consists of but one letter, and a letter normally silent, at that.

The twelfth-century philosopher and rabbi, Moses Maimonides, made a similar point when he insisted that God addressed Moses alone during the revelation at Sinai. For Maimonides, the people at the mountain heard nothing but the loud noises and indistinct sounds of God's revelation; only Moses heard actual words. Maimonides appeals to the Bible for his unique view of the limited scope of revelation. He points out that in Deuteronomy 5, immediately preceding the Ten Commandments, Moses recalls to the people, "I stood between you and God at that time in order to tell you the word of God, for you were afraid of the fire and did not ascend the mountain."

Maimonides also suggests that the voice of God which was then heard by Moses was created just for the occasion of the theophany at Sinai and never heard again. According to this great medieval Jewish sage, God's voice, the bearer of God's word, was most unusual. It was heard only once. Further, according to Maimonides, everything that God's voice spoke was transmitted through the human vehicle of Moses.

By the narrowest rabbinic view, then, we could fairly conclude that all of the Bible is humanly transmitted and the very idea of God's word is unusual and severely limited. As Professor Brown taught me, we speak of God in this unusual and limited fashion frequently. We simply have no other vocabulary. We use anthropomorphism, human description, to describe the ineffable. The Bible refers to God's hand, finger, nose, even God's backside. Maimonides was among the quickest to point out that these phrases are not meant to be taken literally. Nor, then, are the anthropopathisms in Scripture. In many places God is imbued with human emotions, wrath, anger, even compassion and love. Yet to believe that God is literally subject to the same passions as humans is, at least from a Jewish perspective, a severe limitation of theology.

The Rabbis address this directly when they ask, "How can the Torah command, 'Be Holy, for the Lord your God is Holy?' God is a consuming fire, how can humanity resemble God?" The Rabbis here answer their own question by alluding to the anthropopathisms of Scripture: "Just as God is merciful and compassionate, so you must be merciful and compassionate." Within this context it is clear that the Rabbis took these anthropomorphisms and anthropopathisms as Maimonides explained them, not literally, but as an inadequate means of speaking about the Wholly Other.

For the Rabbis the idea of God's word was but another anthropomorphism. God need not have literally spoken, or if God did literally speak, it was a bizarre and unusual occurrence, heard only by one man and then translated by him for all subsequent generations. The Rabbis could not subscribe to the fundamentalist myth that the entire Bible was literally the word of God. For them, God's will was communicated through that most mysterious and imperfect of vehicles, human discourse. Yet they still believed that within the revelation at Sinai lay the seeds for interpreting that discourse. To the Rabbis, revelation did not happen once, on Sinai, but continually, through the ongoing interpretation of Scripture. In this lay the paradox of revelation. The Bible was not in its entirety literally the word of God, eternal and inerrant—yet it served as the source of authority for the continuing revelation of Sinai, which takes place in the ongoing dialogue between the Book and its readers.

Chapter Three

RABBIS AS READERS

The long, slow ascent of the elevator in the classroom building of the Jewish Theological Seminary gave rise to an occasion in my theological education. I was witness to a confrontation between an otherworldly, bookish, pious professor and a senior rabbinical student about to be unleashed on an unsuspecting Jewish community. This student had a reputation for never preparing for his classes, and not because he was so brilliant there was no need to. This joker simply had a very high embarrassment threshold and was unfazed session after session when he made a fool of himself before his classmates.

"You know, Professor," said the student, oblivious to his mentor's cringe, "I'm graduating this May."

"I know," lamented the professor.

"You know," the student continued, "here I am, finishing my seventh year of rabbinical school here, and just recently I realized that I don't know anything."

"I know," returned the professor with no change in his tone.

"But, you know, it finally dawned on me," the student blathered on. "Why should my congregants listen to me?"

At this the professor wheeled around on the student, trapping him in the corner of the elevator. This teacher, normally hunched over his books, now pulled himself up to his full height of over six feet and literally screamed at the would-be rabbi in the narrow confines of the elevator, *"Because you tell them so!"*

With impeccable timing the doors to the elevator slid open at the top floor and the professor turned heel and marched out. I exited as quickly as I possibly could and turned to see the doors close on the student, who now began his descent. For the first time in my life I understood the term "ashen complexion."

Later that day I saw the rabbinical student in the cafeteria. Though I had never spoken with him I felt compelled to go over and offer a word of consolation.

"I saw what that professor did to you in the elevator earlier today. I'm really sorry," I began, but he cut me off.

"You know," he said, "I've been here seven years, in what's normally a six-year program, and today was the first practical thing I learned about being a rabbi."

I was confused by his response and asked him to explain. "The professor was right to do what he did and say it the way he said it. That's the whole ball game. Only the force of personality gives us clergy any power. Only by instilling fear, or at least the will to listen to the rabbi, can Judaism have any authority in this day and age. He taught me the secret I needed to know; now I can be a rabbi."

The moral of this story is no secret to any clergy member, nor to any congregants who sit on the boards that hire and fire. The authority of the clergy no longer rests in the Bible which he or she wields. The authority of religion only extends as far as the first time a member of the flock says no. What is astonishing is that this isn't merely some twentieth-century postenlightenment phenomenon. Millennia ago, shortly after the destruction of the Second Temple in Jerusalem, the Rabbis confronted this reality.

When the Jerusalem cult was destroyed by the Romans in 70 C.E., the sacrifices spelled out in Leviticus came to a halt. The insistence of Deuteronomy, that the Jerusalem Temple be the exclusive place where God's name would rest, now became a dilemma in the face of Roman troops tearing down the city and plowing the rubble into the soil. How was a theology which proclaimed God universal to find authority in a Scripture which consistently mandated blood sacrifices in a now defunct Temple?

In the decades following the destruction of the Temple and the concomitant stripping of authority from the words adrift on pentateuchal parchment, the Rabbis set about to reconstruct. What they reconstructed was not the Temple, but rather a Judaism which generated the careful and critical view of the Bible outlined in the previous chapter, and a means of interpreting that Bible in order to keep it alive beyond the sacrificial cult. This means of interpretation was called Oral Torah, and as I recounted in Chapter One, it was proposed as part of the basic package from that point onward. After the destruction assured that blood sacrifice and the system of the written Torah could no longer be efficacious, Oral Torah filled the breach and kept the written Torah viable. Once religious authority ceased to be vested in the Temple and as a result ceased to be vested in the Bible that promoted that Temple, authority moved from the Word to the readers of the Word.

Even as they appreciated the changes which the destruction of the Temple spelled for Judaism, the Jews of the first century lamented its destruction. In a very canny statement the head of the Jewish community at the time observed, "By rights, since the destruction of the Temple we Jews should all be in a state of semimourning, and so the Rabbis should decree that no Jew eat meat or drink wine as a sign of that mourning. However, it is a principle that the rabbinic court will only decree prohibitions which the people will follow."

This statement is astonishing for many reasons, not the least of which is that its author, Rabban Shimeon ben Gamaliel, actually said it for the public record. In speaking about the destruction of the very locus of religious authority up to the first century, Rabban Shimeon recognizes that the people, as a corporate entity, have replaced the Temple as the source of authority in Judaism. For the Bible and the ongoing injunctions it contains to remain alive, that viability must be tested continually in dialogue between the interpreters of Scripture and their congregants.

What Rabban Shimeon is pointing to is the fact that for Judaism, much as for Christianity in the late first century, the Temple ceased to be a source of authority in biblical religion. Even more startling, but true in both sister religions, is that in some ways the Bible itself ceased to be an authority. Stated more accurately (and less paradoxically) the Bible remained a source of authority only through the ongoing interpretation of the documents it contained.

A very good example of the eclipse of the Bible's role may be found in the foundation document of rabbinic Judaism, the Mishnah. This work, edited in about the year 200 C.E., replaced the biblical narrative with a system of rabbinic opinions arranged anthropologically in categories such as Agriculture, Calendar, and Torts. While other rabbinic documents consistently cite Scripture as the source of authority for the opinions, both legal and theological, found in them, using the catchphrase "As it is written . . . ," the Mishnah seems to bend over backward to avoid quoting from the Bible. It is as though the editor of the Mishnah, Rabbi Yehuda the Patriarch, declares his independence of the Bible. No longer can authority be construed "as it is written"; a new source of religious authority is now found in the words "Rabbi X says."

Even this is not so simple as it first seems, for Rabbi X, Y or Z was always ready to buttress the force of his pronouncements with a verse of Scripture if called upon to do so. The development of scriptural exegesis alongside and contemporaneous with communal case law guaranteed that the apodictic forms of the Mishnah (such as "Rabbi X says") found their counterparts in scriptural prooftexts ("As it is written"). One is all the more impressed with Rabbi Yehuda the Patriarch's deliberate avoidance of Scripture in the opening paragraphs of his Mishnah.

The text, from the order on agriculture and the tractate on benedictions, presumes that one is wholly familiar with the customs of the Jewish community. In other words, the Mishnah is not a cookbook or primer for Judaism; it presumes one knows how the system works. And, as we will see when we look at even one brief example of text, it is not exactly a law code either. First of all, it glories in contradictory opinions, laid out side by side. Second of all, and contrary to the dictates of the justices of U.S. courts, the Mishnah seems to believe that hard cases make interesting and even good law.

Now the book of Daniel in the Bible already records that it is the custom in the Jewish community to pray three times a day: morning, afternoon and night. And Deuteronomy 6:7 refers to recitation of certain verses "when you lie down and when you rise up." The Rabbis presume those verses to be the paragraph in Deuteronomy 6 which contains that command, a paragraph that opens with the famous words "Listen [*Shema*], Israel, the Lord our God the Lord is One." Hence it was the custom in the Jewish community to recite the Shema morning and night. Enter the Mishnah:

> From what time may one recite the Shema at nighttime? From the time at which the priests enter to eat their special portion until the end of the first watch (in the Temple); these are the words of Rabbi Eliezer. The sages say, Until midnight.

The Mishnah opens with presumptions: that everyone knows that the Shema is meant to be recited as part of the evening liturgy, that the only real questions to be worked out are the time parameters for saying the Shema, and that the opinions that matter are those of Rabbi Eliezer versus those of the sages. The authority here is "Rabbi X says," and not "As it is written." But note how cleverly the Mishnah builds on the unspoken verse of Bible lurking behind the discussion. It presumes that Deuteronomy's command to recite "when you lie down and when you rise up" is universally interpreted to mean liturgical recitation of the Shema. It is presumed that the words "lie down . . . rise up" refer to evening and morning recitation of the Shema and that all that's left is to work out the details. It presumes as well that though the Temple was destroyed 130 years earlier everyone still finds it convenient to set their watches, as it were, by Temple time. Said less politely, the Mishnah co-opts the language and time frame of the Temple cult in order to invoke both the ritual and authority of that biblically enjoined locale. By not citing the verse of Deuteronomy (at least not for a while; it does get quoted, probably much to everybody's relief, in the fourth paragraph of the Mishnah), Rabbi Yehuda the Patriarch replaces the force of "As it is written" with the force of "Rabbi X says." But even as he does it, what Rabbi X is talking about is interpretation of Scripture. The very subversion of written Torah by Oral Torah keeps the Written Torah viable. Phew!

My argument here is admittedly complex and perhaps hard to follow by anyone not familiar with the dialectical methods of rabbinic literature. Let me try to illustrate the point from the other end of the Mishnah to show, again, how the Rabbis insist on Oral Torah as the standard for judging the written text and keeping it alive. A good part of the argument the Rabbis make lies in what is unsaid or presumed.

The scholar Judah Goldin suggests that in the earliest texts of the Mishnah, the collection ended with a tractate of nonlegal sayings, mostly pithy wisdom of the sort that could be found on the lips of every garden variety Stoic anywhere in the late Roman Empire. The tractate is called *Pirqe Avot*, or Lessons of the Fathers. *Avot* opens with a piece of religious-political propaganda which sets about to prove that the sages, Rabban Yohanan ben Zaqqai and his disciples, are the rightful inheritors of rabbinic tradition, and thus are the correct persons to be leading the rabbinic academy following the destruction of the Jerusalem Temple. Much like the philosophical schools of the Hellenists, *Avot* sets out a chain of tradition which establishes an unbroken set of links from masters to disciples—from the founder of the school to the current head, Rabban Yohanan. As head of the academy and rightful inheritor, it is he and he alone who has the privilege of interpreting the traditions of his academy for his disciples:

> Moses received the Torah from Sinai and transmitted it to Joshua. Joshua transmitted it to the Elders and the Elders to the prophets. They transmitted it to the People of the Great Assembly.

The Mishnah's chain of tradition is peculiar. First, it squeezes great gaps of chronology into very few phrases; by the time the chain reaches Rabban Yohanan it will have jumped from Moses to him in but fourteen generations, just like every chain of tradition in the philosophical schools (and the Gospel of Matthew, while we're at it). Second, it conveniently omits certain very important groups from the outline of Jewish history—such as the priesthood. Better to forget them as a recent source of power now that the Temple is no more, n'est-ce pas? Third, and most important, it uses the term "Torah" rather loosely. Rabban Yohanan and his disciples, the publishers of this chain of tradition, do not mean the Pentateuch or the Bible when they speak of Torah here. They take advantage of the linguistic elasticity of the Hebrew term, which literally means "teaching," and so imply that whatever interpretations Yohanan and his disciples are offering have the authority of Moses at Sinai. Last, the terms "received" and "transmitted" are technical terms. Here they refer not to Morse code but to the "traditions of the fathers," those oral interpretations and customs which exist in the community alongside and perhaps independent of Scripture.

This deliberate obfuscation needs to be emphasized. The Rabbis speak here of "Torah from Sinai," but when they do so they do not mean the Bible. We have already seen in Chapter Two that the Rabbis had a far more critical view of the interaction of revelation and Bible to characterize it quite so simply. When the Rabbis speak of Torah from Sinai they mean *their Torah.* In other words—and this cannot be emphasized too strongly, for it was the very nature of the rabbinic perception of revelation which led them to this reading—Torah from Sinai means Oral Torah. The Rabbis insist again and again that it is their readings of Scripture, their interpretations, their legal decisions which now carry the weight of revelation. What happened that fateful day at Sinai when Moses went to receive the Torah? What in fact *did* God say to him? *Leviticus Rabbah,* a fifth-century commentary, suggests that "Mishnah, Jewish law, additional matters, Jewish lore, even what a senior disciple will offer to his master as a novel interpretation, these were spoken to Moses at Sinai." According to this statement, all rabbinic traditions (I suppose even what I am writing on this page) were heard by Moses. All carry the authority of Sinai. All rabbinic tradition is authentic revelation. Is there, then, any limit to the religious authority of the rabbinic interpreter? Yes, the congregation he or she leads determines the parameters of revelation. All the congregants have to do to deny the authenticity of revelation, to nullify interpretation, is "just say no."

The Rabbis, of course, emphasize again and again the power of their reading as revelation. Let us listen to another piece of Mishnah which shows not only how insistent the Rabbis are about their own power of interpretation, but illustrates as well what careful readers of Scripture they were. The text is found in the tractate *Rosh HaShanah,* but deals with the revelation at Mount Sinai:

> Moses ascended [Mount Sinai] along with Aaron, Nadav and Avihu, and seventy elders of Israel. Why are the names of the elders not published? In order to teach you that every court of

three judges which is ever constituted must be considered as though it were the court of Moses.

First, let us consider the cleverness of the observation. The Rabbis were careful readers of Scripture. It did not escape their notice that the Bible offers genealogy lists at the drop of a hat. Genesis is bursting at the seams with "begats." How can it be, then, at this central moment of Jewish history, that the text goes mum? Why is there no list of the seventy who were on Sinai? It seems an unthinkable omission, like a multimillion-dollar wing added to a hospital anonymously. Unless, of course, the silence is meant to teach a didactic lesson. Here's the homily: the absence of the names is meant to make us respect all rabbinic courts, that is to say all future interpreters of Scripture, with the same respect we would afford those seventy who accompanied Moses to receive the Torah from God. Again, Oral Torah has the power and authority of written Torah.

This idea that the Torah Moses received is, in fact, the Torah, or teachings, of the rabbinic readers of the Book, is no more poignantly expressed than in the following story from the Babylonian Talmud (*Menahot 29b*). In its fullest form it is meant to be a Jobian theodicy which expresses the moral that not even Moses was given the privilege of understanding why God allows saints to be martyred. Here, we'll read a shortened version of the tale, for I wish to focus on the exegetical insights of the legend:

> When Moses ascended into heaven to receive the Torah, he found God sitting and adorning certain letters calligraphically, adding crownlets to the letters.

Moses asked, "Master of the Universe, who is preventing you from giving the Torah unadorned?"

God replied, "I have a certain man who will exist many generations from now. His name is Aqiba ben Yosef. In the future he will interpret mounds upon mounds of Jewish law from these very jots and tittles."

Moses asked, "Can you show him to me?"

God replied, "Turn around." Moses found himself in Rabbi Aqiba's classroom, where he went and sat in the back row. He couldn't follow a word of what they were saying and grew dizzy from it all. Finally, they arrived at a difficult point of discussion and when the students pressed Aqiba, asking, "Rabbi, where is your scriptural authority for this?" he replied to them, "This law was given to Moses at Sinai."

Moses felt better so he returned to ask God, "You have a person like this, yet you choose to give the Torah through me?"

God responded, "Shut up! This is My plan."

The first thing we should notice about this remarkable little story is Rabbi Aqiba's argument stopper. When he cannot prove his point to his students, Aqiba, that most ingenious of exegetes, seems to become disingenuous when he simply claims, "This law was given to Moses at Sinai." Generations of impatient teachers have stopped their students' eager queries ever since with the exact same words. But Rabbi Aqiba spoke the truth, for what he heard, at least by the rules of narrative, *was* given to Moses at Sinai. Moses was at Sinai while he was simultaneously in the back of Aqiba's classroom. Thanks to the magic of Walt Disney what Aqiba spoke as law was given to Moses at Sinai.

The story underscores the rabbinic insistence, spelled out above, that what Moses heard at Sinai was Oral Torah, the give and take of Aqiba's rabbinic classroom. Moses did not understand it, to be sure; but he heard it. The content of the revelation may have been beyond him, a mystery, but it was given to Moses at Sinai.

When Moses wonders why an interpretation which leaves him dizzy should be presented under the guise of his authority, God shuts him up. The story makes it clear that as the generations pass exegetical technique will grow so complicated, seem so alien to the original receiver of Torah, that Moses will sit in the last row of the class, with the least bright students. He will be dizzy with incomprehension. The only thing he will recognize and so be cheered by is his own name, invoked by the rabbi as the source of authority for his innovation. The third-century storyteller has made his point: don't expect him to understand it, it's enough for Moses to lend us his authority so we may continue to call our interpretations of Scripture the Torah Moses received on Sinai.

Stated another way, this legend teaches that the Rabbis thought there could be no written Torah without Oral Torah. There is no biblical text without interpretation, for the word of God must be heard by the ears of each and every generation, determined by each community afresh. As the Rabbis would have it, the author of Torah, Moses, is the disciple of the interpreter of Torah, Aqiba. This paradoxic reversal of roles which makes Moses, the Rabbis' teacher par excellence, into the dazed student of Aqiba, presses the point home. The only way to read the Book is to engage it actively. It must grow to something beyond Moses' own comprehension if it is to remain viable. Because it is the Word of God, humanity must interpret it.

The chutzpah of this position is delightfully narrated in a famous story about an oven, told in the Babylonian Talmud tractate *Bava Metziah 59b*. It is, as it were, the rabbinic inverse of Dostoevsky's Grand Inquisitor, a carte blanche for rabbinic freedom of interpretation. The story is lengthy and bears some explaining along the way, so I'll interrupt my own narration to explain and kibitz until all the cards are on the table.

We begin with a man named Ochnai, who wanted to corner the market on ovens in the Jewish community of Palestine in the late first century of the Common Era, shortly after the destruction of the Temple in Jerusalem. Ovens, in those good old days, were made of clay and could become ritually unfit for use (nonkosher, as it were) for a variety of reasons. The catch with earthenware is that once it becomes unfit one's only recourse is to smash it, as there is no way to make it fit for use again. Bad news for the householders of Palestine; good news for the clay lobby.

Enter Ochnai, with an oven made of alternating layers of clay and sand. By the rules of ritual fitness, sand may never be rendered unfit, so it looks like Ochnai's oven may be the neatest bakeware until microwave comes on the scene two thousand years down the road. To ice the cake he's baking, Ochnai's proponent in the rabbinic academy arguing his case before the decisors of Jewish law is none other than the famous Rabbi Eliezer ben Hyrcanus, known to his colleagues as Rabbi Eliezer the Great.

As the story goes, on the day they argued the case in session, Rabbi Eliezer gave every conceivable argument in the world, but his colleagues didn't accept his opinion. It has been suggested in this century that the Rabbis disagreed with Eliezer in order to protect the Jewish clay workers' interests, but that's a matter for economists of late antiquity to decide. In any case, our story continues with Rabbi Eliezer making last-ditch arguments to convince the Rabbis of Ochnai's case.

Looking out the window he gestured and said to them, "If

the law is as I suggest, let this carob tree prove it." There is some confusion as to what actually happened at this point. Some say the carob tree actually uprooted itself and moved a hundred yards. Others disagree. They suggest it moved four hundred yards. Nevertheless the Rabbis were not impressed. They said to him, "You can't bring a proof about Jewish law from a carob."

Eliezer tried again and said, "If the law is as I suggest, let this wellspring prove it." Of course, the water in the spring changed its course and began to flow backward. The Rabbis' response? "You can't bring a proof about Jewish law from a wellspring."

Eliezer was undeterred. He said, "If the law is as I suggest, let the walls of the academy prove it." At this juncture the walls began ominously to incline, threatening to fall altogether. Rabbi Joshua, an old sage who was vice chair of the academy rebuked the walls, telling them to mind their own business—which was to hold up the ceiling. "If disciples of the sages are engaged with one another in debate of the law, what business is it of yours?"

The walls were in a tizzy. They couldn't fall out of respect for Rabbi Joshua, but they wouldn't right themselves out of respect for Rabbi Eliezer. And, the Talmud adds with a wink, to this very day the walls of that academy are cockeyed.

Rabbi Eliezer gave it one last try, "If the law is as I suggest, let it be proven from heaven." Sure enough a voice resounded and said, "Why do you argue with Rabbi Eliezer? The law is as he suggests it to be in every instance!"

At this Rabbi Joshua jumped to his feet and shouted (quoting Deuteronomy 30:12), "It's not in heaven!" What, the Talmud asks, did he mean by "It's not in heaven?" Rabbi Yermiah explained, "The Torah was already given at Sinai.

We don't pay any attention to voices, God, because at Mount Sinai You already wrote in the Torah, 'Follow the majority.' "

I have to jump into the story here to point out that Rabbi Yermiah is far more chutzpahdik than he seems, reading *Robert's Rules of Order* to God. He rubs God's nose in it, as it were, by quoting from the Bible that the Rabbis follow majority rule and so Rabbi Eliezer is outvoted, never mind what God's opinion on the matter may be. But his quote from the Bible bears some examination, because it's not quite as elegant as is Rabbi Joshua's "It's not in heaven." Rabbi Yermiah's "Follow the majority," comes from Exodus 23:2 and it pays to quote the verse in full to see what violence Rabbi Yermiah is doing to Scripture as well as to its Author: "Do *not* follow a majority to do evil; do not bear witness in a suit to follow the majority to pervert justice." Rabbi Yermiah is rather guilty of taking his three words out of context. How ironic that at the very moment when the Rabbis assert their right to interpret Scripture, Authorial intention be damned, they justify it by simply breaking a verse of the Bible into pieces. By the time Rabbi Yermiah is done explaining what Rabbi Joshua meant, it seems the Rabbis have cornered the market on exegesis much more thoroughly than Ochnai ever dreamt of for his oven.

This salutory talmudic tale has a number of endings, only one of which is immediately applicable here. Rabbi Nathan, a saintly character who was blessed with visits from the heavenly traveler, Elijah the prophet, once had occasion to ask the latter about God's reaction to this precise display of rabbinic hermeneutical hubris. Elijah reported that God just grinned and said, "My children have outwitted me, my children have outwitted me."

I suppose it's not all that surprising that in a rabbinic telling of the tale the Rabbis should find God tickled by their gumption. The moral of this particular story is clear: God supports rabbinic interpretation of Scripture. Even when the Rabbis do violence to the apparent meaning of the text, interpretation is to be preferred as a means of determining communal practice than reliance on miracles. The Rabbis, who were no slouches at wonderworking themselves, nevertheless frowned on charisma. It was far better to argue from the text, for by their lights, it was the best way to preserve the text.

Rabbi Joshua's quote from Deuteronomy deserves fleshing out in this context, both as it is found in the Bible and as it is understood by the Rabbis:

> The commandment I command you today is not hidden from you, nor is it too far from you. It's not in heaven, that you might say, "Who can go up to heaven for us and bring it down and explain it so that then we might do it?" Nor is it across the sea, that you might say, "Who can cross the sea, and get it for us and explain it so that then we might do it?" The word is very close to you, in your mouth and in your hearts. Do it.

Deuteronomy leaves no room for excuses. God's word is right here with you—do it. For the Rabbis this was not only a charge to perform the commandments, it demanded constant study and interpretation of them. Reading the Book was what kept the word close by, in their mouth and in their hearts. It demanded, by its very placement in those two sites, full engagement of the intellect. In the give and take of communal discussion, in the debate among scholars, in the practice of generations worked out anew again and again, the Bible became a timeless text.

Now that we've spent three chapters together exploring who the Rabbis were and how their particular community viewed the Bible, it's time to turn our attention to their actual interpretations of Scripture. How was the Bible made relevant to their community? What means of interpretation did the Rabbis use that were shared by readers of the Bible in the Church? Were there midrashic means of discussing the Bible which might still be profitable for us today? How can we learn the lessons of past readers so that we have strategies for reading the Bible now?

We begin our survey of interpretations of pentateuchal narratives by considering the longest-running family soap opera in history, the Abraham cycle in the Book of Genesis. Let us see how readers over the centuries have turned a rather morally ambiguous character into Father Abraham, Teacher of Faith.

Chapter Four

FATHER ABRAHAM, TEACHER OF FAITH

. . . .

Picture a grade B boilerplate spy movie. There's desert, famine, a dangerous border crossing. The hero turns to his stunningly gorgeous wife and tells her, "My dearest, you are very beautiful. If they see you and find out you are my wife, they will kill me but keep you alive. So that I may remain alive, tell them you are my sister." Up till now the male lead is unambiguous, protective of his wife, heroic. The couple adopts a pose in order that the husband may survive long enough to fight his way out of the dilemma and into the next scene. We've seen this picture dozens of times on late-night television. But imagine how disconcerting it would be if the protagonist added, "And while we're at it, I'll be able to turn a profit on you."

Now, instead of a hero we might imagine the male lead to be a slimeball, someone who would offer his wife to strangers, sell his virgin sister, offer you dirty postcards, hot wristwatches. Sure enough, as the plot unfolds, the female is recognized to be exceedingly beautiful, and when Mr. Bad is told of her beauty, he takes her to live with him. To ice the cake, the male lead does profit richly. In the way of movies set in the Middle East he is rewarded for the woman with sheep and cattle, mules and donkeys, slaves and camels. Pretty sleazy business; the kind of thing you'd expect from a James Bond clone made with a very low budget, or from Pedro Almodovar at his campiest, no? Well, look again—the plot and dialogue quoted above is from Genesis 12; the male lead is Abraham.

The moral ambiguity of this characterization, the shift in role from the romantic, protective husband to the low-life hustler was felt long, long ago. This reading, while purposely provocative, is not to be dismissed as merely an impious blasphemy of the Holy Bible. First, allow me to translate the text (rather literally) so that you can judge how to read these seven verses of Scripture. Then, I'll share with you some of the discomforts over this passage found in ancient commentaries:

> There was a famine in the land, so Abraham descended to Egypt to stay there because the famine in the land was so bad. When he got near coming to Egypt he said to Sarah, his wife, "Behold, I know how beautiful a woman you are to look at. When the Egyptians see you and ask whose wife is that, they'll kill me and keep you alive. Say, please, you're my sister in order that I might benefit on your behalf, and they'll keep me alive because of you."
>
> So it happened when Abraham came to Egypt that the Egyptians saw that the woman was very beautiful. Pharaoh's officers saw her, praised her to Pharaoh, and the woman was taken for Pharaoh's household.
>
> Abraham profited because of her. He got sheep and cattle and donkeys, slaves and handmaidens, mules and camels.

One of the earliest commentaries on this passage dates from the first century C.E. and was found among the Dead Sea Scrolls. Called the *Genesis Apocryphon* by scholars, its author is terribly uncomfortable with the Bible having Abraham enlist Sarah to lie on his behalf. As a palliative to this discomfort, the retelling of the tale in this Dead Sea scroll has Abraham dream about a cedar and a palm tree. When men seek to cut down the cedar the palm cries out, so the cedar tree is saved by the palm. Abraham awakes from his frightful dream and interprets it for Sarah: "They will seek to kill me but will spare you . . . so tell them, 'He is my brother' and because of you I shall live and my life shall be saved."

Though the moral ambiguity of Abraham is recognized by this passage, it is not solved—only the dream is solved and the blame is shifted to the giver of dreams, God. Placing the responsibility with God is important, for as we'll see, the ancients read these disturbing stories with a keen eye and understood that God functions in a different moral sphere than humanity.

Later rabbinic midrash treats this passage much differently. Glossing over the moral ambiguity, the Rabbis cunningly invent action to keep Abraham on the pedestal of heroism. The point of departure for the midrash (*Genesis Rabbah 40:5*) is notice of the subtly laconic style of the biblical narrative. The first half of Genesis 12:14 reads, "So it happened when Abraham came to Egypt." The midrash asks:

> So where was Sarah? Abraham put her in a crate and nailed it up so no one might see her beauty. When he got to the Egyptian border, the customs officials told him, "Pay duty."
> Abraham said, "Fine, I'll pay."
> They asked, "Are you carrying clothing?"
> He said, "I'll pay for clothing."
> They asked, "Are you carrying gold?"
> He said, "I'll pay for gold."
> They asked, "Are you carrying silks?"

He said, "I'll pay for silks."

They said, "Are you carrying jewels?"

He said, "I'll pay for jewels."

They said, "It isn't possible! Open the crate and we'll have a look at what's inside."

When Abraham pried open the crate, all of Egypt glowed from her radiance.

The fragment from the Dead Sea Scrolls quoted earlier also recognizes the power of Sarah's beauty. Rather than setting a scene, it simply invents dialogue for the Egyptian officers reporting to Pharaoh:

". . . and beautiful is the shape of her face! How . . . fine her hair. How lovely her eyes, pretty her nose and all the radiance of her appearance. How fair are her breasts and how comely her complexion. How comely are her arms, how pretty her hands, her hands are so pretty to look at. How delightful her palms, how long and slender her fingers. How comely her feet, how fine her thighs. No maiden nor bride is fairer than she, she is more beautiful than all other women. She is better-looking than all of them. Further, she has much wisdom along with all this beauty, so whatever she does succeeds."

The Talmud (*Bava Batra 58a*) tells it somewhat less lyrically: "Compared to Sarah, other beauties were like monkeys."

Let us not let Sarah's beauty blind us to the dark side of Abraham's action. We are used to hearing Bible stories in which Abraham is wholly good, and those who play opposite him are wholly evil. Yet, the Bible narrative is not so neatly black and white. Let's rejoin the narrative where we left off. After all, Sarah is now in Pharaoh's clutches. Will Sarah be violated? Worse, might she be seduced? Will Abraham come to the rescue? Worse, might he simply split with the lucre? Stay tuned as we return to Genesis 12:17–13:2.

> So God smote Pharaoh with a great plague, and his household, on account of Sarah, Abraham's wife. Pharaoh called in Abraham and asked, "What have you done to me!? Why didn't you tell me she was your wife!? Why did you tell me she was your sister, the result of which was that I took her as a wife? Now, here is your wife, take her and leave!"
>
> Pharaoh commanded his men about him and they sent him and his wife and all that he had away. So Abraham ascended from Egypt, he and his wife and all he had, along with his nephew Lot, to the Negev. Abraham was very rich in cattle, in silver and in gold.

The Bible offers us a classic *deus ex machina* rescue. God plagues Pharaoh and saves the girl. Our hero returns to the scene to reclaim his wife. Pharaoh gets the Henny Youngman award for saying, "Take your wife, please." When the Rabbis comment on the scene they suggest that Pharaoh's plague was sexually debilitating, at one blow smiting him and protecting Sarah's virtue.

And yet it's not so simple. Reading the biblical text without the assistance of the Rabbis cheering Abraham on from the sidelines, Pharaoh's moral outrage is evident. He was hurt through his ignorance, yet he had acted only blindly, not with malice. One cannot help but think that had he known Sarah to be the wife of Abraham, Pharaoh may well not have touched her—or so at least he protests. Abraham, for all his worries at the border, seems to have misjudged the situation thoroughly. His own moral ambiguity led him to impute base motives to others. But following the implications of this reading, the result of the story leaves us baffled. In the end

Sarah suffers the ignominy of being passed back and forth like so much chattel. Pharaoh, acting in innocence, suffers plague to himself and his household (shades of a later, less innocent Pharaoh). While Abraham, for all his moral ambiguity ("Tell them you're my sister," indeed!), winds up with a hefty profit. Descending to Egypt in famine he ascends from Egypt with the spoils of his trickery.

What are we to make, then, of this biblical narrative? What *is* the moral to the story? Must Abraham always come out on top just because he's the hero? Does it matter how he behaves or is it sufficient that God has chosen him to transmit the covenant? Is the point of all this that God is metaethical? Are ethics just conventions of civilization, pacts between one human and another or between tribes and groups? If so, does God fit into the picture at all, or is God benignly (we hope) above the scene, picking and choosing regardless of behavior or ethics? Are we supposed to see Abraham as a bit sleazy precisely to get this point?

Perhaps we can look at the story another way and assume that Abraham does act heroically. Maybe in the ancient Near East "tell them you're my sister" is perfectly acceptable behavior. Is it not possible that within the tribal structure of biblical times cunning and trickery are worthy traits? Might we not read this and all the other Abraham narratives as examples of "wisdom" and conclude that Abraham deserves the covenant because he has the street-smarts to survive? Is the lesson of the Bible here that "when you're a Jet you're a Jet all the way?" Is it okay to lie and cheat Egyptians if it means you get ahead a little? Can you sell your wife, pawn her off as your sister and still keep God's approval?

This is not a happy set of choices. Either we assume that God and Abraham are acting outside of our modern ethical conventions, or we assume that they act according to a set of conventions entirely alien to the norms of our culture. The Bible is a perplexing text when we attempt to read it as we would any other narrative. It's great fiction by those lights, for it raises endless questions and allows us to use the text as a whetstone for sharpening our moral perceptions.

Read this way the Bible can be seen as the longest-running soap opera in history. It's in its millionth rerun—the story of an ancient dynasty, full of tragedy and triumph, violence and passion, deception and devotion, tenderness and cruelty—except that instead of running Friday nights, it plays on Saturday and Sunday mornings in synagogues and churches coast to coast. As with all good soap opera, we know what will happen to the characters well before they know. In viewing the biblical characters we see ourselves and test our morality against theirs. The trouble with reading the Bible as soap is that it is *canon* and not soap. Generations of religious communities chose to see in it something more, so that in their reading they found spiritual satisfaction and moral guidance.

For two millennia, readers have employed some form or other of midrashic hermeneutic to make this narrative into the story of St. Abraham. When the tale was told and retold, whether around the campfire or from the lecterns of church and synagogue, this became the story of Father Abraham, teacher of faith. To tell this version of the story, the Rabbis began with Abraham's childhood, filling in the gaps in the Genesis narrative. The Bible gives us very little information about Abraham's early years. When God speaks to him in Genesis 12, Abraham is already seventy-five years old. All we know about the previous years is what may be gleaned from a precious few verses of Scripture in Genesis 11:26–32:

Terah lived seventy years and begat Abraham, Nahor and Haran who begat Lot. Haran died before his father, Terah, in the land of his birth, in Ur Kasdim. Abraham and Nahor took women for themselves, the name of Abraham's wife was Sarah, she was barren and had no offspring. Terah took Abraham his son, and Lot, Haran's son, Terah's grandson, and his daughter-in-law Sarah, his son Abraham's wife, and went with them from Ur Kasdim to journey to the land of Canaan. They came to Kharan and dwelt there. Terah was two hundred five years old and died in Kharan.

Now let's listen as the Rabbis put some meat on the bare bones of this plot. We'll want to know more about Abraham's relations with his father, and with his brother, Haran. Haran is important to us not only because of the odd report of his untimely death, but also because his son, Lot, plays Sancho Panza to Abraham's Don Quixote during his wanderings.

Before we let the third-century Rabbis speak, let's pay homage to the laconic narrative power of Genesis. In this seemingly innocent genealogy, similar to dozens of others which dot the Bible, we are given rich detail. The mentions of brothers, nephews, barren wives and travels weave a web of foreshadowing which will carry the narrative of Genesis through the next twelve chapters. For the ancient listeners who had heard the story so many times before, the genealogy reminded them of all the details of the great family saga about to unfold. All the mistakes, all the jealousies, all the sibling rivalries, the deceptions, betrayals and broken promises are hidden in these few lines of genealogy. It is an appropriate vehicle to carry the weight of that family's history, for the genealogy also serves to remind us that it's our own family we're reading about.

The Rabbis turn their attention to their great ancestor with every intention of glorifying him. For the Rabbis it was not enough that Abraham obeyed God's call, they make him a hellenized monotheist, as they were. He is a man who will stand up for his beliefs, even against a ruling power which arrogates for itself the rights of God. In depicting Abraham as they did, the Rabbis delight in parodying the idol worship of their own time. Abraham is not simply a monotheist, but the archetypal iconoclast.

The antipagan picture the Rabbis paint in their depiction of Abraham borrows some of its colors from elsewhere in the Bible. Drawing on the polemic of the Book of Daniel, they make use of the fiery furnace found there. The rabbinic appropriation of the furnace is fueled by a pun, for Abraham's hometown, Ur, can be translated as "furnace." In transposing the theme from one part of the Bible to another, the rabbis offer Nimrod the role of King Nebuchadnezzar. Nimrod serves as their emperor king, and while he draws his personality from the rulers in rabbinic times, his genealogy is listed in Genesis 10:8–10:

> Cush begat Nimrod who was a mighty warrior in the land. He was a mighty hunter before the Lord, which is why people say, "Like Nimrod—a mighty hunter before the Lord." The beginnings of his kingdom were Babel. . . .

These two sets of genealogies are all the Rabbis need to spin their tale. Let's listen to Rabbi Hiyya, an early-third-century Palestinian, as he tells it his way (I'll translate from the Aramaic of *Genesis Rabbah 38:13*):

> Terah was an idol maker. Once upon a time he went somewhere and left Abraham selling idols in his stead. A man came to buy one and Abraham said: "How old are you?"

He answered, "Fifty something."

Abraham retorted, "Woe to a fifty-year-old who would bow to a one-day-old!" The man left ashamed.

One time a woman came carrying a platter of flour. She asked Abraham, "Can you offer this before them?" Abraham got up and took a club in his hand and smashed the idols. Then he put the club in the hand of the largest remaining idol.

When his father came home he asked, "Who did this!?"

Abraham said, "Why hide it from you? A lady came carrying a platter of flour and asked me to offer it to them. One said, 'I'll eat first.' Another said, 'I'll eat first.' Then this big fellow picked up the club and smashed them!"

Terah said, "Are you kidding me? Do these have intelligence!?"

Abraham countered, "Can't your ears hear what your mouth says?"

[In his anger at his son's insolence, Terah] took him and handed him over to Nimrod.

Nimrod said, "Bow to fire."

Abraham replied, "Better I should bow to water which can extinguish fire."

Nimrod: "Bow to water."

Abraham: "Better I should bow to clouds which carry water."

Nimrod: "Bow to clouds."

Abraham: "Better I should bow to wind which disperses clouds."

Nimrod: "Bow to wind."

Abraham: "Better I should bow to a human who can suffer wind."

Nimrod: "You talk too much. You'll bow to fire because I'm going to throw you into it. Let your God come and rescue you."

Haran stood there undecided. He said, "What the hell, if Abraham wins I'll say I'm with Abraham. If Nimrod wins I'll say I'm with Nimrod."

> When Abraham descended into the fiery furnace and was
> saved they asked Haran, "Who are you with?"
> Haran said, "I'm with Abraham."
> They took him and threw him into the fire and his guts were
> scorched. He staggered out and died in front of his father,
> Terah, which is why it is written, "Haran died before his father,
> Terah."

This peach of a tale does so many lovely things at once.
Formally and technically, it explicates (though in a baroque
fashion) the difficult verse of Scripture which reports Haran's
death. Now we understand that as he lived like a hypocrite,
with an outer demeanor that did not reflect his inner turmoil,
he also died like a hypocrite, with his innards burnt but his
mortal shell apparently intact. The tale lampoons idol makers
and worshipers who know perfectly well what these statues of
wood and stone may be, but worship them anyhow. Abraham
the iconoclast is all the more impressive, for he rejects the
very idolatry he grew up with. Knowing his father to be the
creator of the idols rather than vice versa was sufficient for his
rebellion.

A much later midrash plays out Abraham's childhood dis-
covery of the truth of monotheism, again using Nimrod as
the foil. Here, the text draws on the slaughter-of-the-in-
nocents motif found in Exodus about Moses and reiterated
about Jesus in the Gospels. It offers the delightful picture of
Abraham as bar mitzvah boy, happily recognizing the reason
for his coming-out party:

> When Abraham was born, the mighty men of Nimrod's court
> sought to kill him. He was hidden underground for thirteen
> years. During this time he saw neither sun nor moon. After
> thirteen years he came out of his solitary hiding place. He spoke

Hebrew, rejected idolatry and had faith in his Creator, saying, "Happy is the person who trusts in the Lord of Hosts" (Psalm 84:12).

Here Abraham is an autodidact, learning the theological truths which the Rabbis promote and doing so in Hebrew! A fourth-century sage offered a platonic parable to help understand how monotheism was intuitively obvious to Abraham:

> Rabbi Isaac said, It is like a person traveling from place to place who came across a castle ablaze with lights. He asked himself, "Is it possible this place could have no master?" Sure enough, the owner appeared and said, "I am the master." So Abraham asked, "Is it possible that this world has no master?" God appeared and said to him, "I am the Master of the world."

The second-century sage Rabbi Shimeon ben Yohai (of whom another midrash reports a thirteen-year stay hiding in a cave) offered an even more ingenious explanation for how Abraham came to learn the truth of monotheism. The rabbi is reported to have said:

> Abraham's father did not teach him. Nor did Abraham have a rabbi. How did he learn this essential teaching of Torah? God appointed his two kidneys to be two teachers and they taught him wisdom. This is why it is written in Scripture, *I bless the Lord who gives me counsel; in the night my kidneys instruct me* (Psalm 16:7).

Rabbi Shimeon deftly explains this seemingly bizarre verse by applying it to Abraham's particular situation of being the only monotheist in a world of idolaters. In fact, Rabbi Shimeon trots out an anatomy of humors well known in the ancient world and shared by the Psalmist. The kidneys were thought to be a seat of wisdom in the body, and for Rabbi Shimeon, there was no more valuable wisdom (which he characterizes as Torah) than knowledge of the One God.

A brief pause is in order here to comment a bit on the Rabbis' midrashic hermeneutic, for by now we've seen enough of their invention to appreciate their method. First, the Bible collapses in on itself. Everything serves as commentary on everything else. Daniel's fiery furnace can serve as a set for a scene in Abraham's life. A genealogy mentioning Nimrod can provide the necessary heavy for the cast of characters. Verses of Psalms can serve as commentary on Abraham's actions or even as dialogue to be placed into Abraham's mouth. Anachronism abounds as time telescopes inward so that early and late have no relation to one another. Platonic metaphor can be found in Abraham's mouth as readily as legends once associated with Rabbis are told about biblical characters.

The spaces between the lines of the Bible are filled in orally with dialogue which provides the characters with the traits, background and theology that the Rabbis wish they'd had. Finally, those irritating passages of Scripture which betray an ethic or morality not quite in keeping with the Rabbis' own are either glossed or glossed over. The irritant is either smoothed away or, in the elegant words of Professor Shalom Spiegel, made to serve as the grain of sand around which the pearl of midrash is formed. These operations assist the transformation of a character of morally ambiguous nature into St. Abraham. In transforming this character, the community of rabbinic readers accomplish much more. They make the character called Abraham speak to their own needs and their own generation. In doing so they make the narrative called Genesis into a canon of sacred Scripture, the Bible.

The Rabbis provided Abraham with a full life as a monotheist. He not only served as an opponent of polytheism in their legends about him, Abraham also actively spread the good news of One God throughout the ancient Near East. Now there is little explicit material in Scripture which shows us how Abraham went about seeking converts. For that matter, there is virtually nothing in the Bible that would even lead one to assume he did seek converts. While we're at it, I am hard pressed to think of a verse or verses from the Abraham story that even demand him to have been a monotheist (though the Rabbis presume that like any good Jew he observed the commandments, so he *must* have been one). But what may not be explicit may certainly be implicit. The Rabbis are not beyond eisegesis when their ideology calls for it. (*Eisegesis* is the opposite of exegesis—the latter means literally "bringing out" or inferring something from the text, while the former means "bringing in" or introducing something to the text which is not already there.)

The sages of the Midrash find an opening early on in the Abraham narrative. Genesis 12:1 is the real beginning of the cycle, for it is there God commands Abraham, "Get up and leave your land, your birthplace, your father's house and go to the land I will show you." Abraham so dutifully follows God's orders that four verses later we are informed, "Abraham took Sarah his wife and Lot his nephew and all of the property they had amassed and the souls they had made in Kharan and they went forth to go to Canaan. . . ." It is here the exegetes drive their proselytizing wedge. The third-century rabbi Yose ben Zimra notes:

If you gathered all of the creatures in the world to try to create a mosquito, they still couldn't fling a soul into it. And you tell me Scripture says of Abraham and company, "the souls they made in Kharan"? So who are these souls? These are the converts they made. If so, then why doesn't the text say "converted"? What's the point of "made"? It teaches that anyone who makes a convert out of an idolater is as though he had created him anew. So, why does it say "they made" and not "he made"? Rav Huna explained: Abraham would convert the men while Sarah would convert the women.

Now that we've found some scriptural evidence for Abraham's proselytizing, we will watch his character be developed by the Rabbis with a sensitivity to his status as a desert dweller. Though the Rabbis tended to be urban, they lived in a time and place where the wanderings of the Bedouin were yet well known. The fierce rule of Semitic hospitality was assumed of Abraham, particularly since the Bible itself gives evidence. Genesis 18 tells the story of Abraham's visitation by three angels and his elaborate hospitality to them. We'll return to that story at the end of the chapter, but for now let us watch how second-century sages read that hospitality into other aspects of Abraham's life:

"Abraham planted a tamarisk tree in Beersheba . . ." (Genesis 21:33). Rabbi Yehuda interpreted this verse to mean that Abraham planted an entire oasis so that anything a traveler might ask for would be found there for him: dates, figs, even pomegranates. Rabbi Nehemiah disagreed and said that Abraham opened an inn so that anything a traveler might wish for would be there for him: cold cuts, wine or eggs.

We see how the Rabbis can disagree with one another in their efforts to show the extent of Abraham's hospitality, while simultaneously showing us their own preferences of palate. A century later another Palestinian sage picked up where his predecessors left off and commented on the second half of the verse, fusing hospitality with proselytism:

> "Abraham planted a tamarisk tree in Beersheba and called there on the name of the Lord, the eternal God." Rabbi Shimeon ben Laqish said, It should not be understood that "Abraham called" [Hebrew: *vayikra*] but rather that Abraham caused others to call [*vayakri*] on the name of the Lord. Rabbi Shimeon said that Abraham made every passerby speak of the Holy, praised be He. How did he do so? After they ate and drank and wished to thank Abraham he would say to them, "Was what you ate really mine? Give thanks and praise to the Creator of the World."

A century after this story was spun, an even more elaborate version combined hospitality and proselytism with a further rabbinic assumption about Father Abraham—he was the institutor of rudimentary statutory prayers. In the mid-fourth century Rabbi Azariah told it this way:

> When, thanks to Abraham's hospitality, a passerby would eat or drink, he'd tell them, "Pray." When they asked, "What shall we say?" he would have them recite, "Praised is the Eternal God from whose beneficence we have eaten." If they prayed they went on their merry way, but if they refused to pray Abraham would present them with a bill:
>
> | | |
> |---|---|
> | One pint of wine | $10 |
> | One pound of beef | $10 |
> | One loaf of bread | $10 |

Then Abraham would ask them, "Who gave you wine in the wilderness? Who gave you deli in the desert? Who gave you bread in the broad expanse?" When they saw how pained he was, they, too, took pains to proclaim the faith through proper prayers.

So far as the Rabbis can read into the text, Abraham teaches his dinner guests how to say the grace after meals. By means of a pedestrian pun, the Rabbis can also credit Abraham with introducing the first of the three daily prayer services which Jewish law requires. Genesis 19:27 reads, "Abraham arose early in the morning to go to the place in which he had stood before God." The Talmud (*Berakot 26b*) comments that the word "stood" refers to the daily statutory prayer, often referred to in rabbinic parlance as the Standing Prayer, after the posture which is assumed for its recitation.

This betrays a certain lack of vision at the same time it displays the sages' penchant for cleverness. Abraham goes to stand before God in the place where he had bargained unsuccessfully to try and save the city of Sodom. There can be no more poignant expression of the dynamics of spontaneous prayer than Abraham's haggling with God over the fate of that city. That is to say, the Rabbis could have happily held Abraham up as an example par excellence of what prayer is all about and how to do it—even when unsuccessful. Instead of seizing upon this example, the Rabbis narrow their scope to the fixities of organized religion and prescribed prayer. Emphasis is placed on Abraham's early rising to "prove" that he instituted the morning service, thus assuring the observant that their daily ritual has a venerable history.

This is carried even further in the ninth century when a midrash (*Pirke Rabbi Eliezer*, chapter 27) sees Abraham as the inspiration for the precise formula of morning prayer which the Rabbis would coin so many centuries after his death. God tells Abraham in Genesis 15:1, "Fear not, Abraham, I will shield you." In the rabbinic reading of the text, the angels in heaven chorus in response the very liturgy which is still found in Jewish prayerbooks: "Praised are you, God, shield of Abraham." This is the first of the rabbinically authored Eighteen Benedictions, the backbone of each of the three daily liturgies. We'll see in the next chapter how through a violent retelling of Genesis 22, the same midrash credits Abraham's son, Isaac, with the second of those benedictions.

Before we move on to Isaac, however, it is worth a moment to savor Abraham's transition from discoverer of the One God to Father of Faith. We will devote most of our attention in the next chapter to showing how the Rabbis depict Abraham's fathering of Isaac and Ishmael as prototypical of the way in which all three religions of the Book look to Abraham to legitimize their spiritual lineage. But let us listen to another lesson learned along the way, a lesson of diplomacy and tact—and of the small value the Rabbis placed on truth-telling as an absolute virtue—taught by the very angels who bear the tidings of a son for Abraham and Sarah.

The story of Genesis 18 tells us first how Abraham bows to the angels, washes their feet and feeds them heartily. Then the visitors, first checking that she is not present, announce that Sarah will bear a son. Sarah overhears this from where she is standing at the tent flap—but let's allow the Bible to continue:

> Now Abraham and Sarah were old, getting along in years, Sarah had even ceased having "the way of women." So Sarah laughed to herself, saying, "After I'm worn out, now I'll have

such an event?! Besides, my husband's so old." God spoke to Abraham: "Why did Sarah laugh saying, 'Shall I truly give birth, what with my being so old?' Is anything too wondrous for God? Next season I will return to you when she is birthing —Sarah shall have a son."

In the cosmopolitan city of Caesarea in the late second century the sage Bar Kappara expounded:

Household peace is a mighty thing, for Scripture has told a white lie here in the Torah for the sake of peace between Abraham and Sarah. For Sarah said, "After I'm worn out, now I'll have such an event?! Besides, my husband's so old." Yet when God reported it to Abraham it was discreetly altered in order not to insult him, so it says, "What with *my* being so old."

How careful a reader is Bar Kappara and how keen of him to notice the discretion of Scripture. Abraham's feelings are spared, God reports only that Sarah worries about her age and not that she laughs at the possibility that the old codger might still father a child with her. In any event, we've come a long way from "Tell 'em you're my sister." So let us discreetly withdraw from the delicacy of this household moment, and turn to the offspring of Father Abraham.

Chapter Five

BINDING ISAAC

"Call me Isaac." Some years ago—never mind how long ago precisely—he took to introducing himself that way to everyone he met. He led with his name, laughter in his voice, to distance himself from his splenetic, grim-mouthed half brother. That other was a wild man, his hand against every one, knocking people's hats off in the street. The brothers could not circumambulate the city of a dreamy Sabbath afternoon. When Isaac was with Ishmael there was sport, but never any rest.

Poor Isaac, always in the shadow of his hulking thirteen-year-older brother. The butt of his jokes, the unwilling recipient of his untoward affections. Poor Ishmael, who endured his baby brother's scorn until the elder was banished from the hearth completely, even if not from a place in his father's heart. Woe to them both, for the rivalry for their father's love and for the love of their Father in heaven, which set them against one another all their lives.

It cannot have been easy for Ishmael to endure. He, too, was a child of promise. Before he was ever born God promised his mother, Hagar, that her seed of Abraham would be most plentiful, uncountable in number. To his father, Abraham, God said of Ishmael, "I have blessed him, I will make him very fruitful and increase his numbers greatly. He will bear twelve princes and become a powerful nation." Even after Sarah bore Isaac and insisted that the rival and her son be banished, God promised Abraham, "The son of the handmaid will I also make into a nation, for he is your offspring." And like his cousins the Israelites, who were enslaved in his mother's native Egypt, Ishmael could claim, "God hearkened to his voice." When God attended to the thirsty Ishmael, languishing in the desert, God's angel announced to Hagar, "Lift up the boy, grasp him with your hand, for I shall make him a great nation." Yet for all of this Ishmael knew, for daily was he reminded, "My covenant is with Isaac."

Nor could it have been easy for Isaac. Despite God's promise to his father, Abraham, the covenant was in Ishmael's flesh as well as in his own. Although the command came to Abraham to "circumcise every male among you at eight days of age, for all generations," in his zeal to obey God's command,

> Abraham took his son, Ishmael, and all who were born in his household, as well as all whom he had acquired by purchase, all the males in Abraham's household, and circumcised the flesh of their foreskins on that very day that God had spoken with him. Abraham was ninety-nine years old when he circumcised the flesh of his foreskin. His son, Ishmael, was thirteen years of age when he circumcised the flesh of his foreskin. On that very day were Abraham and Ishmael circumcised.

Woe to Isaac and Ishmael, for it is the nature of male rivals to compare the prowess of certain organs. What a contest these half brothers must have had. It is probably better not to imagine too vividly the nature of their digs at one another, the comparisons they may have made. Yet when the Rabbis turn to Scripture they cannot resist conjuring up certain moments of the sibling rivalry centered exactly where we would prefer to avoid looking. And, of all the precipitants which might give rise to rabbinic reactions to the subject, the inverted oedipal moment of the binding of Isaac provides the textual riddle, and so the locus for the brothers' boastings.

We will return later in this chapter to a fuller reading of Genesis 22, that marvel of minimalist narrative. For now, let us join the Rabbis in their trouble over an obscurity in the introductory phrase, "So it happened after these matters that God put Abraham to trial . . ." (Genesis 22:1). It is in the first words of the story that the Rabbis find their occasion to cross into the realm of midrash. "So it happened after these matters" begs one to ask, Which matters? The word "matters" even provides a clue to the answer, for it is one of those lovely biblical Hebrew words with a broad range of meaning.

"Matters" (devarim) can also mean "things" or even better, "words." One could legitimately read this verse of Scripture to mean, "So it happened after these words." Words? What words? Who said what to whom? What could have been said to provoke God to put Abraham to trial? Did Abraham commit some theological faux pas that provoked God to test him so cruelly? Was there some command of God he did not fulfill with sufficient alacrity that God had to test Abraham's zeal? Or were there, perhaps, other actors in this drama whose words might have set the trial of Abraham in motion? Later we will ponder the exact nature of the binding of Isaac, but for now, let us share the lopsided grin of irony as we see how the Rabbis of Genesis Rabbah find the words which mattered enough for God to put Abraham to trial:

> Isaac and Ishmael were quarreling. Ishmael claimed, "I am more beloved than you, for I was circumcised at thirteen years of

age." Isaac responded, "I am more beloved than you, for *I* was circumcised [at the commanded time] at eight days old." Ishmael replied, "I am surely more beloved, for I could have prevented it, but I did not." At that moment, Isaac blustered, "Would that the Holy, praised be He, be revealed to me and tell me to chop off one of my limbs, I would not prevent it!" "So it happened after these *words* that God put Abraham to trial. . . ."

How clever of the Rabbis to introduce the narrative of Genesis 22, the binding of Isaac, with the dialogue of vicious sibling rivalry imagined here. The brothers' banter takes a dangerous tone as each boasts that his circumcision is more lovable. What better prelude to a father inexplicably raising a knife, at God's command, once more. The Rabbis telescope the entire bitter family history into this one verse which now not only serves as the proem to the binding, but alludes to the rivalries which will dog its interpretation for millennia afterward.

There are yet other readings of the verse which point to both the entire compass of the biblical family saga and to its subsequent interpretation. A ninth-century Aramaic translation of the passage takes the liberty of expanding it for our edification. Before we listen to the translator perform during the weekly Sabbath Torah lection, let's recall what informs his ingenuity. When Sarah's handmaid, Hagar, bore a son to Abraham in her mistress's stead, the potential role reversal of barren mistress and fecund maid sufficiently threatened Sarah that she demanded of Abraham, "I placed my handmaid in your breast, now that she is pregnant shall I be diminished in her eyes? May God judge between you and me" (Genesis 16:5). When Abraham gave Sarah free rein to do with Hagar as she wished, the handmaid fled the household.

At the command of God's angel and with the promise of a child named Ishmael, Hagar returned to submit to Sarah's oppression. It was unrelenting; so much so that when Sarah bore Isaac, she ordered Hagar out of the house. The matter hurt Abraham terribly, yet he succumbed to God's command which proclaimed, "All that Sarah tells you, hearken to her voice, for it is through Isaac that your offspring shall be reckoned" (Genesis 21:12). How did Sarah make her demand? "She said to Abraham, 'Expel the handmaid and her son, for the son of that handmaid will not inherit with my son, Isaac' " (Genesis 21:10).

Now that we've caught up with the ruthless singlemindedness of Sarah, let us return to the ninth-century synagogue where the Aramaic translator is about to offer his new, improved version of Genesis 22:1.

"It happened following the words" exchanged by Ishmael and Isaac as they battled one another. Ishmael said, "It is fitting that I inherit father since I am his first-born son." Isaac said, "It is fitting that I inherit father since I am the son of his wife, Sarah, while you are but the son of Hagar, my mother's maid." Ishmael responded, "I am more worthy than you, for I was circumcised at thirteen years of age, had I wished to prevent it I would not have risked my life to be circumcised. You were but eight days old when you were circumcised. Had you any knowledge of what was happening perhaps you wouldn't have risked circumcision." Isaac responded, "Today I am thirty-seven years of age. If God asks for all of my limbs I would not refuse." These words were heard by God and so, immediately the word of "God put Abraham to trial. . . ."

Here, the boasting over circumcision takes a back seat, at least initially, to the clue provided by Sarah's rage. The real story is about who will inherit Daddy. This very real family motive will become a metaphor for the religious traditions' claims of authenticity in the centuries to come. But, before we turn to those various readings of the Aqedah (the binding of Isaac) by Judaism, Christianity and Islam, let us pause a moment to ponder one quirk of mathematics in the Aramaic translator's invention of Isaac's age.

One may readily understand how making Isaac into a mature adult changes the valence of the Aqedah from a test of Abraham to a joint test of both Abraham and Isaac. No longer is Isaac the innocent lamb led to slaughter, he is now a knowledgeable participant in the event—as willing as was Abraham to be a martyr for God's glory. Yet why precisely thirty-seven? Why not the round number forty, or fifty, or simply the consoling thirtysomething? Where does the Aramaist get his math from?

Here again the mother provides the answer. The Rabbis presume a certain order, on occasion, in the unfolding of biblical narrative. Though seemingly episodic, there is method in the seams which stitch the episodes to one another. If Genesis 22 tells of the Aqedah, Isaac's binding and near death, then Genesis 23 may well be viewed in causal relationship to that narrative. The chapter opens with the notice of Sarah's death: "Sarah's life was one hundred twenty-seven years of age. Sarah died at Qiryat Arbah which is Khevron in the land of Canaan, and Abraham came to eulogize Sarah and to mourn her."

Now, suddenly, the mathematics seem simple, though the rabbinic suppositions of causality are admittedly more complex. If the Aqedah was linked, somehow, to the death of Sarah, all we need do is subtract to find out Isaac's age at the time of his binding. Sarah bore Isaac when she was ninety and

she died at 127, hence Isaac must be thirty-seven at the time of
her death. Though there is nothing in the biblical story line
which demands that this juxtaposition be causal, for the
Rabbis it is mete. What has the Aqedah to do with Sarah's
death? The Rabbis are of two minds. In one scenario, the
sages imagine Satan the gleeful bearer of the news that Abraham has put a knife to Isaac's precious throat. In the other
scenario, Isaac innocently returns from the binding to tell
Sarah of father Abraham's fortitude in the face of God's command. In either version, all we hear from Sarah is the death
rattle of Genesis 23:1–2.

Indeed, biblical scholar Phyllis Trible has repeatedly
pointed out that Sarah's voice is audibly absent from the
entire Aqedah narrative. Where is the wife who laughed
when she heard she would bear a child at ninety? Where is
the mother who defended her son's patrimony so fiercely that
she demanded Hagar and Ishmael's banishment? Could Sarah
have sat idly by as Abraham walked off to the mountains
with that mad gleam in his eye, a cleaver in his hand and Isaac
in tow? Could wily Sarah have managed no more than to
have a stroke and die at the news of the Aqedah? Isn't there a
reading of Scripture which places the matriarch side by side
with Abraham during the trial for the life of the son of the
promise?

The Rabbis, alas, fail to provide Sarah with a voice audible
enough to reach us after all these years. But, in the byways of
Christian tradition there are yet some echoes of the voice of
that daughter of virtue and faith. I wish to begin with a
rereading of the story which finds some consonance with the
rabbinic interpretation. In the sixth-century text that follows,
as in the rabbinic midrash cited above, Sarah ends her invented role in Genesis 22 by dying off in preparation for

Genesis 23. Let us listen as the Greek liturgical poet Romanos melodiously gives Sarah back her voice.

While Romanos tunes his lyre, let me pay my debt to my colleague at Oxford University, Dr. Sebastian Brock, who so carefully over the past two decades has introduced these Greek and Syriac traditions to the English-speaking world (in the pages of the Belgian journal *Le Muséon: Revue d'études orientales*). I rely here on Brock's translation from the Greek of Romanos. I also gratefully depend on his publication of Syriac manuscripts and his translation of the anonymous poetry which here follows Romanos's presentation of what Sarah might have said had she known what Abraham was setting off to do:

> If He who first gave the child takes it back, why did He offer him at all? Do you, old man, leave what is mine with me, and when He who called you wants him, He will reveal it to me. He who first of all indicated his birth by means of an angel will again reveal to me his death. I will not entrust the child to you; I will not give him to you.

Romanos has provided Sarah a speech worthy of her fierce characterization in the Bible. She will stand up for Isaac, she will bar the way, even if God does command Abraham. Now the father, who on previous occasion has been warned by God to hearken to Sarah's voice, is baffled. To whom shall he listen? He responds to Sarah's hypothetical speech by pointing out to her that God "has the power to slay him even in your arms. Therefore show your willingness and send him off." Sarah now agrees to the Aqedah and through Romanos speaks to her son, Isaac:

If He desires you for life, He will give orders that you live; He who is the immortal Lord will not kill you. Now I shall boast: having offered you as a gift from my womb to Him who gave you to me, I shall be blessed. Go, then, my child, and be a sacrifice to God, go with your father—or rather your slayer. But I have faith that your father will not become your slayer, for the saviour of our souls alone is good. As you leave your mother, you will find your true father, God the Lord of all. He will reveal to me that you are alive, after you have been slain; even if it is not in the present, He will reveal it in the future. Embrace me who bore you, Isaac, and though I have not received the full joy of my pains of labor, do you both set off.

Not only has Romanos given Sarah the mettle we might expect of her from the Genesis narrative, he has provided her with an attribute we saw imagined for Abraham in the last chapter: she is the mother of faith. Here, she displays faith in bodily resurrection, a motif which the Rabbis, too, associate with the Aqedah. With that faith to give her hope, we return to one last couplet from Romanos to bring Sarah's speech to a glorious end:

When Sarah saw Isaac return unharmed with Abraham, she rejoiced to receive him back again. "May He who has shown you to me once more now receive my spirit."

Now Sarah has died with dignity in full knowledge of and agreement with the Aqedah. The reading of Sarah into the biblical narrative has carefully straddled the fence of credulity, for it simultaneously presents a mother's objections to her son's potential slaughter while offering a picture of Sarah as a pious daughter of monotheistic faith. This tradition is roughly contemporary with the rabbinic midrashim found throughout this book, and it is possible that Romanos has some now-lost midrash as an inspiration. It is equally possible that the Christian traditions on the Aqedah influenced the rabbinic readings of that story (a thesis which we will explore more explicitly later in this chapter).

At the moment, however, I wish to explore another set of homilies which may have been sources for Romanos's genius. Two Syriac verse homilies on the binding of Isaac were published by Dr. Brock in 1986. He suggests an indirect influence of these homilies on the text we have already seen. The voice of Sarah we are about to hear dates from the mid-fifth century and is in Syriac. Brock raises the possibility (most unusual in the surviving ancient interpretive traditions) that the text may have been written by a woman. It will help us further understand the full characterization given to Sarah in what follows. I have taken the liberty of joining the two homilies into one narrative, which I will interrupt on occasion for the sake of transitions and comment.

We open with mother Sarah watching Abraham set off on a journey with Isaac:

> Sarah saw and terror seized her, and she spoke as follows: "Where are you taking my only begotten? Where is the child of my vows off to? Reveal to me the secret of your intention and show me the journey on which you are both going. Never has there been a time when I held you back from the performance of what is good. Have you ever brought in the poor and I have not looked upon them like you? For some of the poor whom we have received have turned out to be angels: they can testify to my mind if what you had in mind was not the same as me. You went off and fetched a calf, while I kneaded unleavened bread: we were as one person with a single love when we received supernal beings, when they were rested and gave us rest

—and the child came as a result of their blessings. But now when you have in mind a journey, why is the child going with you, and why are you not revealing your secret to Sarah your faithful wife who in all the hardships of exile has born trials along with you?"

Abraham puts Sarah off with the promise that he wishes but to slaughter a lamb. He tells her he will bring back the fleece. Sarah replies:

> "If it is a sheep you are wanting to see to, be off and see to the sheep, and return; leave the child behind lest something happen and untimely death meet him, for I am being unjustly deprived of the single son to whom I have given birth. Let not the eye of his mother be darkened, seeing that after one hundred years light has shone out for me. You are drunk with the love of God —who is your God and my God—and if He so bids you concerning the child you would kill him without hesitation."

Thus far we hear the voice of a compassionate and suspicious mother. She does not trust Abraham; his faith is too well known to her—he is "drunk" with it. But again, the dilemma of the interpreter is foisted onto poor Sarah, for she must not merely be a compassionate mother, she must be the mother of faith. Listen, then, as the narrative turns into a competition between the two parents for the attention of their Father in heaven:

> "Let me go up with you to the burnt offering and let me see my only child being sacrificed; if you are going to bury him in the ground, I will dig the hole with my own hands, and if you are going to build up stones, I will carry them on my shoulders; the lock of my white hairs in old age will I provide for his bonds. But if I cannot go up to see my only child being sacrificed I will

remain at the foot of the mountain until you have sacrificed him and come back."

Sarah took her only child and began to speak with him as follows, words full of wonder and with a groan: "When you go with your father, listen and do all that he tells you, and if he should actually bind you, stretch out your hands to the bonds, and if he should actually sacrifice you, stretch out your neck before his knife; stretch out your neck like a lamb, like a kid before the shearer. See, my son, that you do not put your father under oath when he draws out his knife against you, lest his mind be upset and there be a blemish in his offering. And listen, my son, to the words of your mother, and let your reputation go forth unto generations to come."

This speech to Isaac places Sarah firmly at Abraham's side in her display of faith to God. I suppose, as well, the Isaac of this midrash will have as many years on the therapist's couch deciphering Sarah's speech as he will answering why his father raised a knife to slay him. In any case, the Syriac verse homily now turns to the binding and Isaac's deliverance. Upon their return home, Abraham perversely asks Isaac to wait outside and enters the house content to let Sarah believe the sacrifice has actually been accomplished. Her response?

"May the soul of my only child be accepted, for he hearkened to the words of his mother. I was wishing I was an eagle or had the speed of a turtledove, so that I might go and behold that place where my only child, my beloved, was sacrificed, that I might see the place of his ashes and see the place of his binding, and bring back a little of his blood to be comforted by its smell. I had some of his hair to place somewhere inside my clothes, and when grief overcame me I placed it over my eyes. I had some of his clothes so that I might imagine him, putting them in front of my eyes, and when suffering sorrow overcame me I gained relief through gazing upon them. I wish I could see his

pyre and the place where his bones were burnt and could bring
a little of his ashes and gaze on them always and be comforted."

The homily turns from this heartrending pathos of a mother
mourning for her dead son, to Isaac, entering the room safe
and sound. After welcoming Isaac back to her she prays to
God, who ordered the sacrifice in the first place:

"I give thanks to God who has given you to me a second time; I
do obeisance to that voice which delivered you, my son, from
the knife. I praise Him who saved you from burning on the
pyre. Henceforth, my son, it will not be 'Sarah's son' that people
will call you, but 'child of the pyre' and 'offering which died
and was resurrected.' And to You be glory, O God, for all passes
away, but You endure."

With her last words to Isaac, Sarah takes on the role of name-
changer normally associated with God and angels in the Bible. Abraham's name was changed from Avram, Sarah's from
Sarai. Isaac's name here takes on new meaning as his role in
the interpretive literatures of church and synagogue changes
from that of son to symbol. No longer shall he be, indeed,
"Sarah's son," or even son of Abraham. Isaac is now the
inheritor of Abraham and, as such, a metaphor for authenticity in Abrahamic religions.

When the anonymous Syriac homilist has Sarah call Isaac
the "offering which died and was resurrected," it subtly opens
the door to Christian theology with its promise of a dying
and yet resurrected God. That theology looks both backward
to the Hebrew Bible and forward to the bodily resurrection
of all flesh. Belief in Christ as well as belief in bodily resurrection is an act of faith. Already the authors of the New

Testament looked back to the Aqedah as a type of that faith. The Epistle to the Hebrews 11:17–19 evokes such faith:

> By faith, Abraham being tested offered up Isaac, for having received the promise was able to offer up his only begotten son; of whom it was spoken, "In Isaac shall your offspring be called." By reckoning that God was able to raise [corpses] from the dead, he got him back—in parable.

I've translated this passage rather literally to show how the device of typology—reading the "Old" Testament in light of the "New," was already functioning in Hebrews. The reference in the passage to "only begotten son" refers more to Christ than to Isaac. The "in parable," at the end of the verse is a clue to Christian readers that the passage is meant to represent more than it says on the surface. The point is that by faith in Christ one may also have faith in a future bodily resurrection. How may one learn "faith in Christ"? The first-century author suggests the following interpretation: Look to Scripture, it is there that theology is authenticated. Evocation of the Aqedah serves as typological "proof" for the good news of the Gospel. The Syriac homilist uses Sarah, mother of faith, to quietly press home this same point.

It seems that from the time of the New Testament onward the Aqedah became the battleground for answering the question, Who inherits Abraham? The New Testament and Church Fathers were relentless in their reading of the binding of Isaac as a prefiguration of the crucifixion and resurrection of Christ. St. Augustine of Hippo, writing in the early fifth century, takes up this theme in his *City of God* (xvi:32) when he turns his keen hermeneutic eye on the Isaac and Ishmael narratives. Allow me to paraphrase his interpretation:

Abraham could not have believed that God wants human sacrifice, so he is to be praised for his belief that God would resurrect Isaac from the dead after he had been sacrificed. Abraham knew, since God had told him, "Through Isaac will your offspring be called." What does this mean, since Ishmael is also called Abraham's offspring? It means that the sons of promise, and not the sons of flesh, are called descendants of Abraham, and they are those who are gathered in Christ.

Augustine argues for belief in resurrection and suggests that this belief was taught by Abraham at the Aqedah, much as the Syriac homilist presumed it taught by Sarah. But Augustine argues further, by contrasting Isaac and Ishmael, that faith in Christ means being Abraham's authentic descendant. In other words, and Augustine here simply states an argument that Christian interpreters of Scripture had been making since the time of St. Paul, the true inheritors of Abraham are Christians. He carries his analysis into the heart of his reading of the Aqedah, for he makes a specific equation between bound Isaac and Jesus:

Of whom was Isaac a type? It can only be of him who the Apostle says, "He spared not his own son but delivered him on behalf of us all." As Jesus carried his cross, so Isaac carried the wood for his sacrifice. . . . Who was the ram caught by its horns in the thicket? Who, then, but Jesus, crowned with Jewish thorns before he was offered in sacrifice.

Without dwelling on Augustine's blaming the Jews for the crown of thorns (see Mark 15:17—it is the work of Roman soldiers), it is worth admiring his use of typology. Everything in the story points to Christ. Not just Isaac, but even the ram attests to the truth of Christianity. Up until the nineteenth century this was the standard Christian reading of the binding of Isaac.

Nor are the Christians alone in reading the story of Genesis 22 through such particularistic glasses. The prophet Muhammad received, among his revelations from the angel Gabriel, a specific teaching about the binding of Abraham's son. The tale is recounted in the Koran, chapter 37. There the story begins with a brief account of the legend of Abraham smashing the idols (which we saw earlier, in Chapter Four). It is followed by an account of the binding in which both son and father seek to do Allah's bidding. What the angel Gabriel neglected to tell the prophet, however, was the name of the son who was bound. By now it will be no surprise to readers that Muslim commentators for more than a millennium have presumed the bound son to be Ishmael, eponymous ancestor of the Islamic peoples. Just as in the case of Christianity, the Muslim assumption seems to be that identification with the bound son authenticates that religious tradition as the inheritor of Abraham. If it was Ishmael who endured with Abraham, than Islam is the beloved son and dear to Allah.

The Rabbis were no strangers to this sort of polemical exegesis of Scripture. When they read the binding of Isaac they identified wholly with the boy who had the knife at his throat. Jewish history from the fourth century onward reinforced this identification. The Christian conquest, as it were, of the Roman Empire made Jews feel the knife all the more. Once Islam had firmly established itself in the Mediterranean basin and the battle between Muslims and Christians for world domination began in earnest, rabbinic identification with the bound son took on a note of defiant desperation. Recall, if you will, the Aramaic reading of Genesis 22 quoted above, which had Isaac and Ishmael arguing about who was more fitting to inherit Abraham. By the ninth century, when that text found the form in which we read it yet today, Isaac was plainly a stand-in for rabbinic Judaism and Ishmael for Islam.

The ninth-century rabbinic midrash *Pirke Rabbi Eliezer* devotes an entire chapter to retelling the Aqedah. In it, all the actors are on stage: Judaism, Christianity and Islam. We have already seen how conveniently both Judaism and Islam refer to their ancestors as symbols of the religious groupings. Christianity also attempted to identify Isaac as a symbol for Christ. But in this rabbinic rendering of the story, Isaac can only be the Jews. Christianity, unusually, is represented as Abraham's servant, Eliezer. Before we dismiss this representation as a twentieth-century fancy of interpretation, let us recall that Christian texts regularly invoke the servant motif (particularly from Isaiah) as a symbol of Christ. Even more compelling for this interpretation, Eliezer is represented in Genesis 15:2–3 as a potential successor to Abraham. The choice of Eliezer is apt, for God assures Abraham that his true offspring, and not his servant, will be his inheritor.

It seems to me further, that the midrashic storyteller is battling with certain Christian doctrines, particularly those found in Paul's letter to the Romans, chapter 4:1–11:

> What shall we say the father of us all, Abraham, has found according to the flesh? Abraham has a boast if justified by works, but not with God. What does Scripture say? "Abraham had faith in God and it was accounted to him as righteousness." . . . This blessing, is it but on the circumcision or is it also upon the uncircumcision? We say that for faith Abraham was reckoned righteous. How was it reckoned? In circumcision or in uncircumcision? Not in circumcision, but in uncircumcision;

and he received the circumcision as a sign of the faith he had while yet uncircumcised, that he may be a father of all them that believe.

Paul has made two distinctions, one profoundly Jewish, one uniquely his own. The first is between the circumcised and the uncircumcised. It is a distinction to which not only Rabbis but Muslims, too, would heartily assent. The second, Pauline distinction is between faith and works. For the Rabbis, there is no better proof of faith than works—they are one and the same.

We are now ready to read *Pirke Rabbi Eliezer*'s version of the Aqedah.

The Tenth Trial:

Well, maybe we're not quite ready to read, since we yet need some further background. Earlier we saw how the opening phrase of Genesis 22, "So it happened after these matters," gave rise to a series of interpretations about the precise nature of those "matters" or "words." A very old tradition links this with the following phrase in the verse "God put Abraham to trial," and concludes that there were previous trials. Among the various invented trials for Abraham were some we saw in our last chapter: he lived in an underground cave, he endured Nimrod's fiery furnace. *Pirke Rabbi Eliezer* counts these as the first two of Abraham's trials, and continues enumerating them until it reaches the ultimate trial of the Aqedah—the tenth. Before we return to the narrative of that event, it is worth noting what this midrash counts it as the penultimate trial.

In the immediately preceding chapter *Pirke Rabbi Eliezer*

lists the expulsion of Ishmael as the ninth trial. There is a remarkable sensitivity here to Abraham's anguish. Our midrash not only captures the father's tone of despair in the biblical story, but it offers a very real authenticity to Islam as an Abrahamic religion. There can be no doubt that Ishmael represents Islam in *Pirke Rabbi Eliezer*. In that midrash when Ishmael takes a wife he marries Fatima. It happens that Fatima is the name of Muhammad's daughter; she was the only of his children to have offspring and so carries on the prophet's direct line of descent. There could be no clearer way for a homilist to provide the key to his roman à clef. Once again:

> The Tenth Trial
> "So it happened after these matters that God put Abraham to trial. . . ." God tried Abraham time after time to know his heart, whether he could observe all of the commandments of Torah, as it is said, "[Through your offspring all the nations of the land will be blessed] because Abraham hearkened to My voice and observed My observances, My commandments, My statutes and My teachings" (Genesis 26:4–5).
>
> Ishmael returned from the wilderness to see his father, Abraham. Rabbi Yehuda said, On that same night the Holy, praised be He, was revealed to Abraham and said to him, "Take your son" (Genesis 22:2).

The homilist is very clever here as he rebuts Paul's distinction between works and faith. Christians claim, as we have seen, that the binding of Isaac teaches the virtues of Abraham's faith. Nonsense, says the rabbi, what the Aqedah teaches us is whether or not Abraham would observe the commandments. It is *only* by doing so that he may show his faith. The midrash goes further, for it notices a subtlety of biblical style which demands comment. Many, many readers and scholars have observed the laconic nature of the Aqedah narrative. So much high drama is packed into so few verses. The very power of the narrative lies in what it invites the reader to imagine in the silence that stubbornly sits between the lines of Scripture. Wonder, then, that God's command to Abraham is so very wordy. In an economical text one does not need to hear the redundancies of Genesis 22:2: "Take your son, your only son, whom you love, take Isaac. . . ." *Pirke Rabbi Eliezer* reads an entire dialogue in the pauses after each comma:

> "Take your son, . . ." Abraham said, "Master of all worlds, which son? Do you refer to the son born before circumcision or the son of circumcision?" [Some manuscripts read: the son of circumcision or the son of uncircumcision.]
>
> God said, "Your only son," to which Abraham replied, "This one is an only son to his mother and this one is an only son to his mother."
>
> God said, "Whom you love."
>
> Abraham replied, "I love this one *and* I love this one."

Here the midrashist makes his generosity to Islam most apparent. Just as the Muslims granted Jews a special status in Islamic society as a people of the Book, so our rabbi is ready to admit that both Isaac *and Ishmael* are beloved sons of Abraham. This goal having been achieved, he can return to touting Isaac as representative of Jewish claims to be the true inheritors of Abraham:

> God said, "Take Isaac, and offer him there as a slaughter-sacrifice. . . ."
>
> Abraham rose early in the morning and took Ishmael and Eliezer and his son, Isaac.

Here the homilist has resorted to an old trick of midrashic method. Midrash hates anonymity, so when the biblical text says, "Abraham rose early in the morning, saddled his donkey, took his two servants with him, as well as his son, Isaac . . ." every member of the text must be identified. Abraham is Abraham and Isaac, Isaac. Who are the servants? Well, the biblical narrative leaves us very little option: we only know the names of two other males in Abraham's household: Ishmael and Eliezer. They will, I remind you, serve as stand-ins for Islam and Christianity. But appreciate just how much the midrash hates anonymity as our narrative proceeds:

> "He saddled the donkey"—this is the donkey which is the son of the ass which was created at twilight on the sixth day of creation and later spoke to the pagan prophet Balaam. This is the donkey which Moses rode as he descended into Egypt. . . . This is the donkey which David shall ride in the messianic future, as it says in the prophet Zachariah 9:9, "Rejoice fully O daughter of Zion, give shout O daughter of Jerusalem, behold your king comes to you, righteous and humble, poor and riding on a donkey, the offspring of an ass."

Our preacher has taken the opportunity to introduce the full pedigree of the donkey in the story. It is hardly anonymous, it carries on its back all of world history from the creation of the universe to the messianic advent. Like Augustine's treatment of the ram, this donkey becomes a symbol of salvation:

> Isaac was thirty-seven years old when he went to Mount Moriah, and Ishmael was fifty. A quarrel broke out between Ishmael and Eliezer. Ishmael said to Eliezer, "Now Abraham is offering his son, Isaac, as a bound sacrifice on the altar. I am his first born, I shall inherit Abraham."

Eliezer responded, "He already expelled you like a divorced wife and sent you to the wilderness. But I, his servant, who serves him day and night, I am he who shall inherit Abraham." The holy spirit settled the matter by answering them, "Neither shall this one inherit, nor shall that one inherit!"

What faith the homilist himself displays. Though Judaism is but an afterthought in the wars between Islam and Christianity, this ninth-century rabbi imagines God sending a message of faith in the continuity of Jewish history. Only Isaac shall inherit. But, in order to do so, some very harsh reality must be endured. Despite his faith the homilist is aware that Jewish history is entering a long, dark tunnel. The knife will be at Isaac's throat. Isaac, fully consonant with God's direction of history, offers himself as a willing partner to God's plan and Abraham's trial:

Isaac said to Abraham his father, "Daddy, tie me up, tie my hands and my feet lest I tremble and spoil the sacrifice. Then I would transgress the command, 'Honor your father.' " So he tied his hands and his feet and bound him on the altar and arranged the fire and the wood and arranged him upon them. And he put his foot atop him, as a man does when he's slaughtering an animal, so it won't buck. He flexed his muscles and reached out his hand to take the knife to slaughter his son. . . .

Rabbi Yehuda said, When the sword reached Isaac's throat his soul flew out of his body. When God's voice was heard from between the two cherubs (which would be in the Temple on Mount Moriah in the future), and it said, "Do not lay a hand on the boy" (Genesis 22:12), the soul returned to the body.

Thus did Isaac come to learn of resurrection of the dead, from the Torah! For all corpses will be resurrected in the messianic future. At that moment Isaac opened his eyes and said, "Praised are you, God, who resurrects the dead."

A bleak picture of the near future, indeed. Isaac appears to die of fright from the sword pressed to his throat. The exegete shows his cards when he tells us it's a sword and no longer the knife Abraham carried with him up the slopes of Moriah. It is the sword of the crusades yet to come, the sword of Christian and Muslim pretensions to world supremacy. The preacher expects Judaism to die a near death, at least, and then be resurrected.

The death of Isaac on the altar confounds interpretation of Scripture even as it represents the homilist's view of Jewish history. Isaac only appears to die. With the same faith that allowed Abraham to endure, so may Isaac be resurrected. The Bible teaches its truths to yet another generation of readers. They knew the Bible story spoke of Isaac surviving Abraham's trial intact. They knew, as well, that when he walked down the mountain, he was a different person from the small lad who had innocently ascended. Never could Isaac look again at Abraham in quite the same way. Never could Ishmael, standing helpless at the foot of the mountain, again entertain the fantasy that he would, after all, inherit daddy. Woe to Isaac, woe to Ishmael.

We bid farewell to this complex chapter of Bible text and interpretation with one last satisfying glimpse of the creative rereading of Scripture that *Pirke Rabbi Eliezer* has accomplished. The rabbi has read into the text of the Torah that important tenet of Jewish, Christian and Muslim faith—resurrection of the dead. That accomplished, Isaac has truly inherited father Abraham. The midrash imagined Abraham as author of the first of the statutory rabbinic eighteen benedictions: "Praised are you, God, shield of Abraham." Now, in the minds of rabbinic readers of Scripture, Isaac takes his place in line, for as he rises intact from the altar on Mount Moriah, it is the second of those benedictions that he intones: "Praised are you, God, who resurrects the dead." This is the faith that fuels the scriptural interpretations of all three religious traditions, even as they quarrel over who is the beloved son and inheritor of Abraham.

Chapter Six

JACOB AND SONS
· ·

Isaac, bound upon the altar at Mount Moriah, looked wide-eyed at the cleaver in his father's hand. At that moment, high in heaven, the angels cried and beseeched God to have mercy on those unfortunate creatures, for as the Psalmist says, God should have mercy on human and animal alike. Their eyes overflowing with bitter tears of entreaty, the angels moved God to command Abraham not to touch the lad. But, touched he was, report the Rabbis, for the tears of the angels fell into Isaac's wide, wide eyes and brought him blindness in his old age.

It was a blindness that left Isaac in darkness deeper than that which plagued Egypt. Isaac, who as a youth was blind to his half brother's designs, who as he grew was blind to his father's dangerous devotion to God, who as he married was blind to the corruptions of his brother-in-law, who as he fathered was blind to the petty flatteries of his sons, who as he aged was blind to his wife's preference of one son and her schemes to advance him over the other—truly Isaac could not see. It was a total blindness, as only angel tears can bring.

The darkness which encompassed Isaac envelops the biblical text as well. We never glimpse Isaac on his own; he is always seen through the prism of other characters. He is son of Abraham, father of Esau and Jacob. The one episode where he appears *sans* parents or children, in Genesis 26, he takes his wife, Rebecca, to the land of the Philistine king, Abimelech. There he behaves like a pale reflection of father Abraham and passes his wife off as his sister. Truly, Isaac could not see.

But let us not allow his darkness to occlude our vision of him, for Isaac is the link which carries us from father Abraham to the seed of Israel, the sons of Jacob. To serve as that link, Isaac must marry, bear offspring, be in and of the world. Yet after the blinding events on Moriah (Genesis 22), the demands of walking through daily life must have seemed overwhelming to the bound son. He retreats from the biblical text, doesn't even return home with Abraham from the ordeal. We do not see him again until after his mother's death, when a marriage has been arranged for him by his father, through the mediation of a nameless slave. Where was he all this time? In a moment of sympathy for his depression, rabbinic commentators suggest he retreated to the academy to study, safe in the ivory tower from the vicissitudes of father's cleaver, mother's death, and angels' tears.

While studying at the seminary of his ancestors, Shem and Aber, Isaac was unaware of the future Abraham had planned for him. Father fretted for his passive son, fearing that the fierceness of parental religion might drive the child away, cause him (God forbid!) to marry out. Dear mother Sarah was gone now—it was up to Abraham to see after the child of his old age. As Genesis 24 recounts it, Abraham calls in a slave and makes him take a vow not to let son Isaac marry among the Canaanite girls but rather to seek a wife for him among kinfolk, from the old homeland, which at God's command Abraham long ago had left.

And so, the nameless slave sets off to ensure the continuity of the promise, a bride for the son of promise to bear off-spring who in their turn will beget the vast numbers who will populate the promised land. So many promises to fill with only already shortsighted Isaac to carry the load. No wonder Abraham turns to his nameless slave to help him bear the burden of the promises on which he has once already staked his son's life.

This part of the story has a happy ending, for the slave brings home Rebecca who is a woman who knows her mind and who falls for (quite literally—see Genesis 24:64) her chosen partner. The Bible captures Isaac's passive personality brilliantly in its report of his reaction to his new wife: "Isaac took her into the tent of his mother, Sarah; he took Rebeccah so that she was a wife to him, and so he loved her. Thus was Isaac comforted for the loss of his mother" (Genesis 24:67).

In between his father's plans and his mother's tent remains a marriage not of Isaac's choosing but plotted by a slave. The Rabbis, who cannot bear the anonymity of such a moment, identify the nameless slave with Eliezer, who is mentioned by Abraham in Genesis 15:2. We have already seen in Chapter Five how the Rabbis have Eliezer accompany Abraham and Isaac to Mount Moriah, along with Ishmael, for the Aqedah. Now he will be the matchmaker who strikes a deal in Aram with Bethuel and Laban to bring home Rebecca. For the Rabbis, this Eliezer is meant to play Sancho Panza to Abraham's Don Quixote, for they even introduce Eliezer into the narrative of Genesis 14, when Abraham gallops off to rescue his nephew Lot in the "war of the four kings."

That otherwise anomalous narrative, where Abraham is characterized, in the words of Professor Yohanan Muffs, as a "noble warrior," teaches us a good bit about how differing communities read the Bible. It baffled the Rabbis, and their contemporaries the Church Fathers, how Abraham could muster the 318 household warriors he captained. Where, suddenly, did these numbers come from? How was it that this wily iconoclast had such a large number of troops? Ironically, both church and synagogue used the same method to arrive at different answers to this conundrum.

In Chapter One, I wrote about the varying hermeneutic assumptions which the ancients brought to their sacred literature and how those strategies for reading may differ radically from our own. I need to remind readers of that point now, for both the Rabbis and the Church Fathers invoke a startling technique to explain Abraham's troops. It happens that in both Greek and Hebrew the letters of the alphabet also serve to signify numbers. If, for a moment, we pretend not to know how Roman numerals work (if you can remember), or even how Arabic numerals work, we may imagine an entirely different set of numbers based on the English alphabet. A would equal 1, B = 2, C = 3, up to J = 10. Then we would move to tens: K = 20, L = 30, and so forth. Then hundreds, until we ran out of letters. Finally there would be repetitions and combinations of letters to represent numbers in the thousands and larger. Hebrew and Greek used exactly this system (which is retained in the Jewish religious calendar to this day) to signify their numerals.

This numeric technique offers a bizarre hermeneutic tool since every word in Hebrew or Greek also has a numerical value. This valuing is called *gematria* in Greek, with the term borrowed into rabbinic Hebrew. Using gematria, words may be equated with one another. One word which adds up, say, to fifty, may be equated hermeneutically with another word which also adds up to fifty. In this fashion words and numbers can rather freely be interchanged for their "equivalents," making a verse refer to something else altogether. Now we're ready to see how the Church Fathers and Rabbis used gematria to solve the problem of Abraham's warriors in Genesis 14:14.

In a text which dates to around the turn of the first century of the Common Era, the Apostolic Church Father Barnabus (ix:8) writes about Abraham's 318 young household troops. He comments on the inverted ordering of the number in the Greek (and original Hebrew) text of the verse:

> It says, "From Abraham's household eighteen men and three hundred." What knowledge, then, was given to him? Learn that he mentions eighteen first and after a bit three hundred. So far as the eighteen, ten equals *iota*, eight equals *eita*. Together these equal [the first two letters of the name] Jesus. And because the cross was to be graced with the form of the letter *tau*, he says three hundred [which is its numerical equivalent].

Barnabus has used the equivalencies of gematria to "prove" that Abraham rode off to war with faith in the crucified Jesus; that was all the army he needed. All in all, an unusual way to "solve" the appearance of 318 warriors in Abraham's camp.

Let us listen as the Rabbis use the same technique, this time in a more direct form of numerical correspondence. An early-third-century sage, Rabbi Shimeon ben Laqish, suggested quite simply that 318 was the mathematical total of the letters *aleph* (one), *lamed* (thirty), *yod* (ten), *ayin* (seventy), *zayin* (seven) and *resh* (two hundred). What do they spell? Eliezer!

So it is Eliezer who, in the rabbinic imagination, is the unnamed servant who accompanies Abraham on his mission to rescue nephew Lot from his captors. It is Eliezer, the faithful servant who would inherit Abraham, were it not for Isaac.

It is Eliezer who, the Rabbis think, accompanies Abraham and son to the trial at Mount Moriah. Who else, then, but Eliezer could Abraham entrust with the delicate task of finding a wife for his precious Isaac?

That Eliezer takes his charge seriously is indicated not only by the oath by which Abraham adjures him at the outset of Genesis 24, but by Eliezer's careful plotting of a test to find the girl worthy of Isaac. Eliezer is blessed when God has Rebecca offer water to him and his animals, according to the conditions of his devising. The servant is so impressed with the alacrity with which God rewards his mission that he repeats, in full detail, the test he has devised and how Rebecca has passed it when he meets her brother Laban. The telling of the test and its fulfillment is central to the chapter, which comprises sixty-seven verses of narrative, opening with Abraham's desire to marry off his son and closing with Isaac taking Rebecca into mother Sarah's tent. The penultimate verse of the chapter winks at us as it reports that Eliezer repeated for Isaac all that came to pass in order for him to present the young master with his new bride. As we listeners steel ourselves to hear the story yet once more, the report is mercifully limited to that one verse. We do not have to hear the servant recount yet again his triumph.

Although Eliezer brings home the bride, the Rabbis of the Talmud (*Taanit 4a*) are shocked at his behavior. It is not so much the arranged nature of the marriage that distresses them, nor even that Abraham, who was getting on in years, should send a mere servant. It was the test of Eliezer's devising that upset the sages; it made them uncomfortable to watch helplessly as the biblical narrative recounted so repeatedly how that servant had put God on the spot. Some requests simply

should never have been made. As the early-fourth-century
Rabbi Shmuel bar Nahman explained:

> Three made inappropriate requests of God. Two God answered
> appositely, the third God answered with equal impropriety.
> They are Eliezer, Abraham's servant; King Saul the son of Kish,
> and Jeptha of Gilead. How was Eliezer inappropriate? He said,
> "And, when the girl to whom I say, 'Tip your pitcher . . .'
> (Genesis 24:14). She could have been a cripple! She could have
> been blind! But God responded to him appositely and sent forth
> Rebecca.
>
> King Saul, son of Kish, said regarding the challenge by the
> Philistine Goliath, "The man who smites him shall the king
> enrich with great wealth and give over his daughter to him and
> make his family free men in Israel" (1 Samuel 17:25). Saul
> spoke inappropriately, for the man who slew Goliath could
> have been a slave! He could have been a bastard! Yet God
> responded appositely and sent him David.
>
> As for Jeptha of Gilead, he offered to sacrifice to God "that
> which comes forth from the doorway of my house" (Judges
> 11:31). It could have been an animal unfit for sacrifice! God
> responded to him equally inappropriately and Jeptha's daughter
> came forth. Of this the prophet Jeremiah (8:22) lamented, "Is
> there no balm in Gilead? Is there no healer there?"

Rabbi Shmuel bar Nahman was a well-known exegete. His
careful culling of scriptural examples and his zeal for God's
welfare are to be appreciated. He keenly has distinguished a
difference between ordinary requests of God, even urgent
prayers, and the expectations for performance here. In each of
these three cases it is not explicit prayer per se which seems to
be at issue in the biblical narrative. Yet Rabbi Shmuel has
correctly noted that acting as each of these three men has done
is a form of prayer. In each instance, through incredible short-

sightedness, they have laid their futures hostage to quirks of fate or—from the biblical perspective—to acts of God. And so God answers Eliezer, Saul and Jeptha, each according to the divine whim. Through God's grace, and so it was recognized by Abraham's servant, Isaac gains his bride, Rebecca.

Like the matriarch Sarah, Rebecca is reported to be barren. Isaac, for all that he is shortsighted, understands that matters such as these lie firmly in God's hands. With the miracle of his own birth as sufficient model, he entreats God's assistance in curing his wife's childless status. God answers without demurral and as in the modern world, when fertility is sought, Rebecca finds herself carrying twins. When the pregnancy grows difficult Rebecca asks, Why me? God informs her that the twins are destined to spawn two separate nations (shades again of Abraham's offspring), and after a bit of brotherly wrestling in utero, Esau and Jacob appear on the scene.

Here is not the place to rehearse the bitter rivalry between the brothers. We've seen such animosity before in their parents' generation. Suffice it to remember that a famished Esau is forced to sell his birthright in order to share his brother Jacob's bowl. But even before that terrible bargain, we can see the future of the brothers laid out before Rebecca and the readers by God's oracle, "There are two nations in your belly, two peoples from your womb shall part . . ." (Genesis 25:23).

Jacob and Esau carry the burden of literary characters, for they interact not only with all the awful animosities of brothers set against each other, but as eponymous ancestors of entire nations, Israel (Genesis 32:28) and Edom (Genesis 25:30). The drama is carried on artfully in Genesis, for as an individual, Esau-who-is-Edom leads a rich and complex life. His relationship to Jacob is subtle, his reactions to his tricky brother a powerful mix of brute passion and impotent pathos. As a character, Esau may well be more interesting than Jacob. At the narrative's opening we see a loutish hunter with interest in nothing more than his belly. By the time the brothers reunite after some two decades of separation, though the guilty Jacob still fears for his life, Esau has grown rich, savvy and forgiving. As will his nephew Joseph, after a similarly long separation fraught with similarly guilty fears, Esau falls upon his brother's neck, kisses him and weeps.

But Esau remains the symbol of the hated nation, Edom. When the Rabbis read the Bible they haven't a shred of sympathy for Esau. Their reading of the brotherly reunion drips with scorn. What of Esau's hug and kiss? As far as the sages are concerned, when Esau kisses you, count your teeth, and if he hugs you, check for your wallet afterward. Only the late-second-century Rabbi Shimeon ben Elazar has any empathy. He suggests that at that moment Esau's very innards melted and when he kissed his wily brother Jacob, all was forgiven.

Even Rabbi Shimeon's generosity needs some context, for the Rabbis never forgot that Esau was a symbol. Indeed, for them Esau/Edom symbolized the Roman Empire. It is very hard to separate any rabbinic commentary on this passage from their enduring suspicions of Rome, whether pagan or Christian. The Rabbis made their peace with Rome after two or more disastrous rebellions, but they always held their oppressors at arm's length. At best, the sages grudgingly admitted that Rome brought law and order to the empire; they made the trains, as it were, run on time. At worst, Edom/Rome was the last of the temporal kingdoms which would rule over the Jews. It would meet a bitter downfall and then the long-awaited messianic era could begin.

Virtually all rabbinic commentary about the Roman Empire is offered through the guise of exegesis on Esau and Edom. For this reason, we listen with our ears pricked if anyone has anything remotely good to say about Esau. More often than not he is simply a lout, a boor, an unforgiving brother who must always be regarded as having murderous intent. Rabbinic exegesis of Esau is monochromatic—there is no nuance, no recognition of his growth as a character. For the Rabbis, Esau is a character in a children's cartoon, an archetypal bad guy. A story of a certain Rabbi Elazar glibly displays this attitude:

> Rabbi Elazar was sitting in the outhouse doing his business when a Roman came along, yanked him out and sat down in his place! Rabbi Elazar took the loss of his turn stoically, saying, "This cannot be for naught." Immediately, a serpent slithered up from the depths of the outhouse, bit the Roman on his behind and killed him. Rabbi Elazar recited a verse from Isaiah 43:4: "Since you are dear in My eyes, I have honored you; I have loved you and so put a man (adam) in your stead (tahtekha), other peoples in exchange for your life." Rabbi Elazar commented, "Put a man (adam) in your stead": put Edom in your stead.

Instead of lamenting the loss of his dime, Rabbi Elazar turns a delicious pun to celebrate the downfall of his Roman adversary. The fragment of Isaiah he quotes not only allows for adam, a man, to be punned as Edom, Rome, but the end of the phrase is punnable as well. "In your stead," reads in Hebrew as one word, tahtekha, which may equally reasonably be translated (out of context, of course) as "your behind." So a Roman behind was bitten instead of Rabbi Elazar's, and in a twinkle of laughter, Isaiah's prophecy finds fulfillment. As the laughter dies down, we find we have learned all we need to about the Rabbis' attitude toward Esau/Edom, a.k.a. Rome.

Now, having disposed of Esau with a swipe of the hand, I wish to do the same to Jacob as well. The characters in his life, most particularly in his family, become less fully drawn as Genesis progresses. The entire second half of the book shies away from the individual personalities of the patriarchs and moves instead to the representation of Jacob's children as the sons of Israel, a confederation of tribes that will make up a nation.

This is not to say that drama is lacking along the way. For millennia Isaac's words at the time of his son's deception echo in rabbinic ears: "The voice is Jacob's voice, but the hands are the hands of Esau." There is no more severe indictment for hypocrisy. Nor is irony lacking when trickster Jacob finds himself with the wrong sister on the morning after, courtesy of his new brother and father-in-law (Genesis 29). His twenty years of service are a slow repayment for his deceptions of his own brother and father. Jacob's genetic flock management program (Genesis 30) and Rachel's theft of her father's household gods (Genesis 31) seem to be just so much denouement in the family game of tit for tat over the generations.

Brief attention should be paid, however, to the family structure of Jacob, the household of Israel. Somehow Bible-thumping preachers manage to invoke this particular patriarchy as a model of the "right-minded" nuclear family. I am always left a bit shell-shocked when this formulation is piously invoked, for the results of the smoldering sexuality of this father and his children is anything but nuclear, in the family sense of the word. Jacob is hardly a suburban commuter with a wife, two kids, a dog and paneled station wagon. He is a man who fathers a nation, and does so with the sexual scheming of two rival wives and two more concubines. The children he fathers are as full of sexual peccadilloes as the stars of noontime soap operas.

In short order let us mention an eldest son who climbs into bed with his father's concubine. Whether Reuben was merely interested in sexual favors or was plotting an early ascent to his father's throne is incidental. The Rabbis were sufficiently embarrassed by the episode to censor translation of the story when Genesis 35:22 rolled around in the synagogal lectionary cycle. Just a chapter earlier we read of Jacob's daughter Dinah and her rape by Shechem son of Hamor. When Shechem wanted to keep the girl, Jacob acquiesced, providing that the clan of Hamor be circumcised. Jacob's craven behavior is hardly balanced by the brutality of Dinah's brothers, Shimeon and Levi, who ambushed and murdered Shechem's tribe following the circumcision. Their excuse: "Can we let our sister be a whore?" (Genesis 34:31).

Let us recall, too, brother Judah's nuclear family celebrated in Genesis 38. Judah had three sons, Er, Onan and Shelah. Er and Onan shared the same woman, Tamar, serially. Without going into the complexities of levirate marriage and ancient Near Eastern patriarchal laws, we can recall that Judah arranged the marriage of his son Er to this Tamar. When Er "did evil in the sight of God" (Genesis 38:7) and died, Onan, at his father's command, took Tamar to his bed. But Onan, to the eternal shame of his name, performed coitus interruptus with his sister-in-law, so he, too, was put to death by God.

Tamar is to be commended for her pluck. Little brother Shelah was too young to get her pregnant and thus carry on the family name, so she dressed up like a prostitute and hooked father-in-law Judah into getting her in the family way. Eventually, Judah owned up that it was he who had unknowingly implanted seed where his sons had only threshed. As a reward for her tenacity Tamar was blessed with twins, one of whom was Perez. If we turn to the end of the Book of Ruth we learn that Tamar's boy was the ancestor of King David, father of the messianic line. There is a powerful lesson here about the utter irrelevance of the fundamentalist nuclear family to God's plan for the unfolding of biblical history.

All of this rampant sexuality is, mind you, confined to but one family. It is the same family into which the beautiful Joseph is born. I will do no more than allude here to that son's confused sexuality, his attractiveness to powerful women and men equally. His relationship with his brothers is even more complex, but we may leave off, for there is more on Joseph in the next chapter. The point is this: there was plenty for Jacob to worry about, and worry he did.

An early-third-century midrash to Deuteronomy 6:4 expounds on Jacob's worries by opening with a Scriptural question:

> Why does it say, "Speak to the children of Israel" (e.g., Exodus 25:2) all the time? We never see "Speak to the children of Abraham" or "Speak to the children of Isaac," just "Speak to the children of Israel." Our father Jacob merited that the Word be spoken to *his* sons because that patriarch worried all his life about them. He would say, "Oy, what if one of my offspring is a bum, just as it happened with my forefathers."

Here the text takes a detour, but it is worth our while to follow it briefly even though it is not an original part of the midrash but was probably added centuries later. I want to show how it leads two rabbis to two different interpretations of the biblical text. Since both these rabbis are very famous and influential exegetes, the ways they read are instructive not only for the history of midrash, but for modern strategies of reading the Bible, as well:

> Abraham gave birth to Ishmael who worshiped idols, as it is said, "Sarah saw the son of Hagar the Egyptian . . . sporting" (Genesis 21:9); that is to say, he was worshiping idols. These are the words of Rabbi Aqiba.

The literalist exegete Aqiba, whom we met in Chapter One, takes what at first blush is an odd interpretation of the verb "sporting." What's bothering the good rabbi is that whatever it was that Ishmael did, it was enough to have Sarah demand that Abraham banish him from the household. This moral difficulty causes Aqiba to look hard at the word "sporting." Aqiba's reasoning is as follows: the same word is found in Exodus 32:6. There the context is quite different and for Aqiba, instructive. In Exodus, Aaron has just built the Golden Calf. He declares the Calf to be Israel's new god and decrees a holiday for the next day. "They arose on the morrow and burnt offerings and brought sacrifices; the people sat down to eat and drink, then they arose to sport." Nothing could be clearer than that the eating, drinking and sporting of Exodus 32 is intimately connected to the sacrifices offered to the Golden Calf. Aqiba's reasoning is by analogy: just as "sport" there meant idol worship, so "sport" in connection with Ishmael must mean idol worship:

> Rabbi Shimeon ben Yohai said, There are four matters which Rabbi Aqiba expounded and I also expound. My views are preferable to his views. He said [that] "Sarah saw the son of Hagar the Egyptian (hamitzrit)" meant that he was worshiping

idols. I say, however, the brothers were rivals (*tzarim*) fighting over the fields and vineyards. When the time came to divide up their father's property, Ishmael said, "I'll take a double portion since I am the first born." This is why Sarah said, "Banish that handmaid and her son; for the son of that handmaid will not inherit with my son, not with Isaac!" (Genesis 21:10). I think my views are preferable to his views.

Shimeon ben Yohai does have a point. He bases his exegesis of Ishmael's "sporting" on two items. The first is the less clear to modern readers. Essentially, Rabbi Shimeon adopts his teacher Aqiba's methodology when he reads the verse. There is an extraneous element in the text. Why say that Hagar is Egyptian if not to teach us something special about the scriptural moment we are experiencing? Rabbi Shimeon reasons that "Egyptian" (in Hebrew, *mitzrit*) carries with it another nuance, that of a troublesome family rival (*tzar* for a male, *tzarah* for a female). The word is used in rabbinic Hebrew to denote a rival wife, precisely the status Hagar pretends to. But it also means just plain trouble (*tzarah*) or an oppressor (*tzar*) in biblical Hebrew. So Rabbi Shimeon plays on the lexical range of the word to illuminate the role Hagar and her son play here in Genesis. They were rivals, they made trouble. What kind of trouble? Here the context answers the question. The very next verse provides Rabbi Shimeon his second point and seems to justify his reading. Sarah demands Ishmael's banishment. What she is worried about is Isaac getting his fair share of the inheritance. To Sarah's mind the only share sufficient for her fair Isaac is the whole pie. Hence, Ishmael has to go. No wonder Rabbi Shimeon is so pleased with the cleverness of his exegesis.

But I should point out that context was a rare banner for

the Rabbis to follow in their reading of Scripture. What
Rabbi Shimeon has done in offering his contextual proof is an
unusual piece of midrash. In fact, in the rabbinic community
it will be close to another eight hundred years before the
context of a verse is taken seriously as a clue to its meaning.
In the world of midrash Rabbi Shimeon ben Yohai is a prodigy. In fact, the legends about him make him out to be a
prodigy in more ways than one.

A clue to Rabbi Shimeon's special status is already apparent
in the text we've just read, particularly once we know that
Rabbi Shimeon is the disciple of Rabbi Aqiba. Given their
relationship, it is an egregious breach of rabbinic etiquette to
publicly disagree with one's teacher. How much the more so
to crow about it! But Rabbi Shimeon is consistently characterized in rabbinic literature as a man with a very high opinion of himself.

Whether this characterization has anything to do with the
real Rabbi Shimeon or is just a device of rabbinic legend
spinning is beyond me. But he's held in wonderful regard in
the legends the sages told about him, like those which subtly
liken him to Abraham when they suggest that he spent thirteen years hiding in a cave. In Abraham's case, he spent thirteen years hiding from the tyrant Nimrod. When Abraham
returned to the world he was a Hebrew-speaking monotheist.
Rabbi Shimeon stayed in a cave with his son, hiding from the
Roman persecutors. Miraculously they were fed on carobs
and survived. One version of the legend has Rabbi Shimeon
say to his son upon emerging from his cave, "My son, just
you and I are sufficient for this whole world to exist." Another version of this tale has Rabbi Shimeon state, "I've seen
men of worth and they are few. If there are a thousand, I and
my son are among them. If there are a hundred, I and my son

are among them. If there are but two, they are me and my
son."

One last Rabbi Shimeon story illustrates both his hubris
and his relationship to Rabbi Aqiba. It is delightful particularly because it notes he spent thirteen years not hiding in a
cave, but studying at Aqiba's feet:

A drama. Rabbi Hannaniah ben Hakinai and Rabbi Shimeon
ben Yohai went to study with Rabbi Aqiba. They remained
there thirteen years. Rabbi Shimeon wrote home and so knew
what was happening in his household, but Rabbi Hannaniah did
not write nor know what was happening in his house. His wife
finally wrote to him saying, "Your daughter is mature, come
home and marry her off. Despite this he did not go."

Rabbi Aqiba had a vision by means of the holy spirit (a
rabbinic euphemism for hearing local gossip!) and said to his
disciples, "Any one who has a mature daughter, go home and
arrange her marriage." Rabbi Hannaniah got the point, asked
his master's permission to depart, and headed home. When he
got there he couldn't find his house, for they had moved. What
did he do? He went to the well and there he waited until he
heard a girl say, "Daughter of Hannaniah, fill your bucket and
be on your way."

He followed her home and burst in after her. No sooner did
his wife see him than she dropped dead! He said to God, "Master of the Universe, this poor woman, is this her reward after
thirteen years of waiting for me?" At that moment her soul
returned to her body.

Rabbi Shimeon ben Yohai said, There are four things which
the Holy, Praised be He, hates, and I'm not crazy about them
either: a man who holds his penis when he urinates, a man who
has intercourse naked, a man who brazenly recounts the private
matters which transpire between himself and his wife, and a man
who bursts into the house suddenly.

This attitude is vintage Shimeon ben Yohai. It is no wonder we can find him so glibly disagreeing with his teacher Aqiba's biblical exegesis. I wonder, if this is an accurate characterization of Rabbi Shimeon, how anyone could stand to be in a room with him. And I'm sufficiently put off by the first of the four things he and God both hate to leave the remaining three disagreements he has with Rabbi Aqiba by the wayside and return, instead, to father Jacob's worries about his family:

> Abraham gave birth to Ishmael, Isaac gave birth to Esau. I worry I might give birth to a bum, just like my forefathers did. Thus it says in Scripture, "Jacob took a vow, saying, 'If the Lord God be with me and preserve me on the way . . .'" (Genesis 28:20). Now could you think for even a moment that Jacob might say, "*If* God gives me bread to eat and clothes to wear . . . *then* shall the Lord be God to me" (ibid.)? And if God did not provide those things, then will God not be Lord? Hence the biblical text teaches in the very next verse, "I shall return in peace to my ancestral home and the Lord shall be my God" (Genesis 28:21); which is to say, no matter what. So why did Scripture phrase the preceding verse to say, "Then shall the Lord be God to me?" What Jacob was praying for was, Would that God please join His name to me so that I might not ever give birth to a bum.

The midrash here is perplexed as to why Jacob seems to make conditions for accepting the Lord to be his God. To the third-century Rabbis, there simply was no choice in the matter. Since they presumed that Jacob, too, of necessity accepted the Lord as his God, what could he have been driving at when he invoked that formula in Genesis 28:20–21? The answer for the Rabbis solves two textual problems along with its theological elegance. Jacob prays that the Lord will cojoin God's name to himself as a means of preventing genetic mishaps. This not only explicates the repetition of both names of God —"the Lord" and "God"—in the verses, it also explains Jacob's name change. Jacob was also called Israel, and the last syllable of that name is theophoric—that is, it contains a name for God, El. When God changed Jacob's name to Israel, he was assured that his offspring would not go bad.

What fed Jacob's worries? Was it merely his ancestry, his unsavory uncle Esau and great-uncle Ishmael who left him in fear? The midrash quite explicitly turns now to what is gnawing at Jacob's guts:

> It says in Scripture, "When Israel dwelt in that land Reuben went and bedded Bilha, his father's concubine, and Israel heard of it . . ." (Genesis 35:22). When Jacob heard about this he trembled and said, "Oy, maybe there is a bum among my sons!" But he was informed by the very mouth of the Holy One that Reuben had repented of his misdeed, for that verse continues, "The sons of Jacob were twelve." But don't we already know that there were twelve sons? Rather, the force of this part of the verse is to teach that by the very mouth of the Holy One, praised be He, was Jacob informed that Reuben had done penitence and so could still be counted among his brethren. . . .

Now Jacob has relief. Despite the peccadilloes of his children, that steamy sexuality we recounted above, they nevertheless were all right. Though he had four wives, twelve sons and uncounted daughters, all of his kids turned out okay. What parent wouldn't be relieved? Now Jacob can die in peace, knowing from the very mouth of the Almighty that he had done his job and broken the family jinx:

So you find that when Jacob was preparing to depart from the world, he called together all his sons and charged each of them separately, as it says: "Jacob called to his sons: Reuben you are my first-born . . . Shimeon and Levi are brothers . . . Judah your brothers shall praise you . . ." (Genesis 49:1–8). After he had charged each of them separately, he spoke to them all together, as a group. He asked them, "Do you, perhaps, have any disagreements with God-who-spoke-and-so-the-world-was?" They answered him, "Listen, Israel our father, just as you harbor no disagreement with God, so we have no disagreements with God-who-spoke-and-so-the-world-was, in fact, 'the Lord our God the Lord is One' " (Deuteronomy 6:4).

It is for this reason that it says, "Israel bowed on the head of his bed" (Genesis 47:31). Not that he literally bowed on the bed, but rather he gave thanks that no bum ever issued forth from his bed. Others say he gave thanks for what had happened in his bed—in other words, he was grateful that Reuben repented for what he had done with Bilha, his father's concubine.

The Holy One, praised be He, reassured Jacob: "All your life you yearned to hear what your sons have just told you. Now your offspring will perpetually recite twice daily, 'Listen Israel, the Lord our God the Lord is One.' "

The midrash closes Jacob's life with the ultimate assuagement of his worries. Not only does God reassure him that his sons turned out well despite their youthful errors, but the Jewish people undertake to reassure their ancestor as well. In the biblical text of Deuteronomy 6:4, "Israel" refers to the nation; for the midrash, the Jewish people are named the sons of Jacob precisely for the liturgical formula which they daily invoke. In a most unusual rendering of the verse, the sons reassure their father by name: "Listen Israel," Shema Yisroel.

Now the Shema prayer, a cornerstone of the morning and evening liturgy, means not only that God's unity is proclaimed, it means that the Jewish people take a vow to their ancestor that they, too, are at one with God. Rest assured, say the biblical exegetes, Israel's offspring ain't bums. In an uncanny insight into what makes religious observance persist, the Rabbis present the one verse of Scripture that comes closest to serving as a credo as a last promise to a dying man. As we turn in the next chapter to Joseph, son of Jacob, we will see that vows to the dying are taken seriously. The vow his sons took for Jacob preserved them as a family, as a nation, and as God's people, through their enslavement in Egypt and beyond.

Chapter Seven

JOSEPH'S BONES
. . . .

Whan Jacob finished charging his sons he gathered his legs into the bed and died, so he was gathered unto his people. . . . Joseph spoke to the house of Pharaoh . . . "My father adjured me to bury him in the gravesite he acquired in Canaan, may I now go and bury my father, then I shall return." Pharaoh spoke, "Ascend, bury your father as you have vowed" (Genesis 49:33–50:6).

According to the Vienna manuscript of the *Tosefta,* a third-century commentary on the Mishna, tractate *Sotah,* Joseph was requited measure for measure:

> Joseph gained merit by fulfilling his vow regarding his father's bones, so when he died none other than Moses tended to him, as it is said, "Moses took Joseph's bones with him, for he had adjured the sons of Israel, 'God will surely remember you, and then you must take up my bones with you from this place' " (Exodus 13:19).

But now we are too far ahead of the game, for in this verse of Exodus just quoted, Joseph is already dead, leaving Egypt with the fleeing Israelites at the Exodus. Let us rewind our tape to his ignominious entrance into Egypt, where he has been bought by a certain "Potiphar, a eunuch of Pharaoh's, his chief chef, an Egyptian, from those Ishmaelites who had brought him down there" (Genesis 39:1).

As the Bible tells it, God prospered Joseph's hand in Potiphar's house, so Potiphar was very pleased with him. As Potiphar advanced Joseph, the household benefited from the abundance of the Lord's blessings, and as an added attraction, "Joseph was handsome of form and pleasing to behold" (Genesis 39:6). Joseph was enormously successful, rising to the top of Potiphar's household. His success continued unabated until Mrs. (Ms.?) Potiphar took one look at Joseph and challenged him: "Lay me" (Genesis 39:7). Here the Rabbis cannot resist a brief but instructive comment on the whys and wherefores of proper seduction.

They compare this scene of an older mistress of the household and her young slave with another famous biblical scene, from the Book of Ruth, chapter 3. The aged, wealthy, and slightly tipsy Boaz is asleep on his threshing floor during the harvest. Enter Ruth, who uncovers his lower extremities and lies down next to him. The midrash continues, providing dialogue where the biblical text is tactfully mum:

"So it came to pass at midnight that Boaz was frightened, and he reached out to find a woman lying at his feet" (Ruth 3:8). "He reached out," and began to feel her hair. He thought to himself, Evil spirits do not have hair. He inquired, "Are you a spirit or are you a woman?"

Ruth responded, "I am a woman."

He asked, "Are you single or are you married?"

She replied, "I am single."

He asked, "Are you ritually fit or are you unclean?"

She responded, "I am fit."

He asked, "Who are you?" (Ruth 3:9).

She replied, "I am Ruth, your handmaiden" (Ruth 3:9).

Rabbi Berechiah commented, Evildoers are so accursed. In the story in Genesis it says of Mrs. Potiphar, "She grabbed him by his clothing and said, 'Lay me'" (Genesis 39:7), like an animal. While here, Scripture says, "I am Ruth, your handmaiden. May you spread your wings over your handmaiden" (Ruth 3:9).

To which Boaz replied, "Blessed art thou unto the Lord, my daughter" (Ruth 3:10).

Now, isn't that a much nicer seduction scene? And one which gives rise to the messianic scion, to boot. But not all of the Rabbis are so quick to assume that what happened that night on the threshing floor was a seduction. Commenting on Boaz's statement but three verses later, "As the Lord lives! Lie down until morning" (Ruth 3:13), Rabbi Yudan explains:

All that night his libido prosecuted him, it badgered him, it sought to seduce him: "She's single and you're single; you want a woman and she wants a man; rise up, have sex with her, acquire her as wife through intercourse."

Finally, Boaz adjured his libido, "As the Lord lives!" While to Ruth he said, "Lie down until morning."

The Rabbis have no illusions about the seductive destructive power of libido, though they also know it can be tamed to perform God's commands. They wisely comment that without libido no man would build a house or have children. Of course, the Rabbis knew that children were their future. In their eyes, bearing children was the first commandment in the Torah, given to Adam and Eve: "Be fruitful and multiply" (Genesis 1:28). If the same force which causes humanity to disobey God can be harnessed to cause humanity to fulfill the first of God's commandments, "Behold, it is very good" (Genesis 1:31).

The Rabbis had no illusions about the power of young Joseph's libido. As they put it, "Is it conceivable that he was seventeen and in full heat and could resist?" In fact, say the Rabbis, that woman came very close to wearing down Joseph's resistance. As the Bible reports her campaign, after Joseph refused her advances out of loyalty to Potiphar and piety toward God, she nevertheless beseeched him daily. Finally, "the day came that Joseph arrived home to do his work and there was no man of the household at home" (Genesis 39:11). *Genesis Rabbah* (87:7) comments:

> "To do his work" (Genesis 39:11). Rabbi Shmuel bar Nahman explains, Quite literally, he meant to do the work she had requested of him. "There was no man" (ibid.). When he was ready to respond, he found himself unmanned.

There is a debate among the Rabbis as to what protected Joseph's virtue at that seminal moment:

> Rav Huna quoted Rav Matna, He saw his father's image and that cooled his blood. Rabbi Menahama quoted Rabbi Ami, He saw his mother's image and that cooled his blood.

Either way, the Rabbis were duly impressed at Joseph's resistance, whatever may have been its etiology. His impotence became for them a sign of divine grace. Now it is most unusual to find a male-dominated literature praising impotence as a sign of grace. But this is no mere macho rationalization after the fact, it is theology. Given the general impotence of rabbinic Judaism in political and military history, Joseph's failure to rise to the occasion was seen as a virtue. He became the epitome of sexual propriety, the Righteous Joseph. God's will was carried out through him here, as elsewhere in the biblical narrative, much as the Rabbis hoped that their lot in history was a manifestation of God's will and not without reason in the divine economy. Joseph became, at that moment in Mrs. Potiphar's house, a symbol for the Jewish predicament.

Rabbi Shimeon of Kintron suggested that because of the merit he gained through this act of resistance to his oppressor, Joseph's bones caused the Red Sea to part. Rabbi Shimeon's proof?

> It says in Scripture of the Exodus, "The sea saw and fled" (Psalm 114:3). It fled through the merit of Joseph, of whom it is said, "She grabbed him by his clothing and said, 'Lay me,' so he left his clothing in her hand and *he fled* outside" (Genesis 39:12).

One flight merits another. Joseph's flight from his rapacious Egyptian mistress merits the flight of the Red Sea before the Israelites fleeing from Egypt. Measure for measure are our deeds requited. This is a principle that powered the ancient Jewish worldview. Both good and evil are repaid measure for measure. Joseph cared for his father's bones, so his own bones were cared for in turn. Joseph fled from Potiphar's wife, so the sea fled at the approach of the Israelites.

The Rabbis presumed that the principle of measure for measure could explain the actions of God throughout the Bible. It becomes a powerful hermeneutic tool, if applied with some panache. With a bit of whimsy, the very rule itself explains the plagues brought upon the Egyptians in the Book of Exodus. I'll quote the ninth-century text *Seder Eliahu Rabbah* (ch. 8) in full, for it explicates the measure-for-measure mentality while taking God off the hook for punishing the otherwise seemingly innocent Egyptian people:

> "Frogs" (Exodus 7:28 or 8:1–15 RSV). Why did God bring the plague of frogs upon the Egyptians? Because they used to command the Israelites, "Go, bring us creeping and crawling animals, that we may be entertained with them as we so desire." So the Holy, Praised be He, brought frogs upon them until their croaking could be heard from within the very bellies of the Egyptians. The frogs would say, *Kav leKav, Kav leKav.* Not only that, but when an Egyptian would go to the outhouse, a frog would jump out and bite him on the behind. There could be no greater plague than that.

We learn from this midrash not only that the Rabbis had a clear penchant for outhouse jokes, but they believed that justice was duly requited in the end. There is no evidence anywhere in the Bible that the Egyptians demanded that the Jews collect creepy crawlers for their entertainment. Animals such as these were considered ritually unclean by the Bible, so there is both a ritual as well as aesthetic discomfort here. But the assumption that the Egyptians made these demands comes from working backward. If you know the punishment, you can infer the crime by simply using the principle of measure for measure. Why frogs? Surely the reason must have something to do with a sin the Egyptians themselves committed using frogs and their ilk.

I've left untranslated, thus far, the froggy sounds reported emanating from the Egyptians' bellies. Unlike our *ribit* or *chugarump,* there is more than onomatopoeia in the sounds the frogs of Egypt made. Their voices, too, were a plague to the Egyptians, for *kav leKav* translates rather simply: measure for measure.

Let us return to the *Tosefta* text with which we began the chapter to watch the Rabbis adumbrate this principle with many biblical applications. The starting point is the *Sotah,* a wife suspected by her husband of committing adultery. Numbers 5 prescribes a rather gruesome trial by ordeal through which her innocence or guilt is established. Since the Rabbis found such a trial anathema to their sense of justice, they used the case of the *Sotah,* instead, to be the homiletical example par excellence of their principle of measure for measure:

> Rabbi Meir used to say, According to the measure a person metes, so will it be meted out to that person.
>
> Thus you find in the case of the *Sotah,* by the measure she meted out, so was it meted out to her. She stood before her lover so that she might seem beautiful to him, therefore the priest stands her before everyone that they might see her disgrace, as it is said, "The priest shall cause the woman to stand before the Lord . . ." (Numbers 5:18).
>
> She braided her hair for him, therefore the priest undoes it. She put makeup on her face for him, therefore her face turns green. She put eyeshadow on for him, therefore her eyes bug out. She pointed to him with her fingers, therefore her fingernails fall off. She showed him her flesh, therefore her garment is torn, to show her disgrace to the congregation. . . . She spread her legs for him, therefore her thighs decay. She took him on her belly, therefore her belly swells. She fed him dainties, therefore her sacrifice is the food of animals. . . . She did this secret . . . unaware that the One Who Sits in the Secret Places of the Universe would pay heed to her and reveal her secret to public

view, as it is said, "Though hateful acts are covered with guile, evil is revealed in the congregation" (Proverbs 26:26).

We can hear our preacher pounding the pulpit, frothing at the mouth with the juicy details of this adultery. There is little doubt that the homilist understood how to captivate his audience with a bit of prurience. But each and every salacious deed is matched with a punishment, measure for measure. The sermon now expands to other biblical examples:

> The people of the flood (Genesis 6:9ff.) exhibited their pride against God through the very beneficence God poured out for them. . . . They said, "What does God do for us but give us a couple of drops of rain? Behold, we have rivers and wells which supply us in both the rainy and the dry season, as it is said, 'A mist came up from the earth'" (Genesis 2:6). The Omnipresent said to them, "With the very beneficence I have given you you turn your pride against Me! By that very means will I requite justice from you!" Thus it says, "Behold, I shall bring a flood of waters upon the earth . . ." (Genesis 6:17).

With a little imagination we can see how the generation of Noah, whom the Bible accredits with all sorts of moral evils, can also be seen to have rebelled against God through water. To an agrarian society such as theirs (and the Rabbis'), water was the chief source of blessing. To take it for granted was to invite divine disaster. God, rather than withhold the source of blessing, pours it out in such abundance that the blessing becomes a curse and the world is flooded. This is punishment measure for measure.

> Egypt rebelled against the Omnipresent, praised be He, by means of water, as it is said, "Pharoah commanded all his people saying, 'Let every male child that is born be thrown into the River Nile' " (Exodus 1:22). Therefore the Omnipresent, praised be He, requited justice from them by means of water, as it is said, "Pharoah's chariots and his soldiers drowned in the sea . . ." (Exodus 15:4).

Here water again serves as the medium for sin and its punishment. The Rabbis could probably have found other sins, given the many punishments the Egyptians endured, as in the case of frogs mentioned above. But the homilist has a sense of unity in his message, so liquid remains the measure.

Now the preacher moves beyond the Pentateuch for other examples of his principle. There is an exciting interplay here between exegesis and eisegesis. It is very hard to tell when the homilist is inserting the principle of measure for measure into his reading of the text. There are times when he seems to have a sublimely keen literary eye in discerning the correspondences between the crime and punishment:

> Samson rebelled with his eyes, as it is said, "Samson went down to Timnah and saw a Philistine woman among the girls of Timnah. . . . He said to his father, 'Take her for me, for she is upright in my eyes' " (Judges 14:1–3). So he was smitten in his eyes, as it is said, "The Philistines seized him and gouged out his eyes" (Judges 16:21).

Here the homilist has taken a biblical hero and shown how he was punished measure for measure. This is a neat piece of exegesis, for it brings a subtlety of literary parallelism to light (Rabbi Judah adds that just as Samson's downfall began in

Gaza, so it ended in Gaza. This midrash also takes what the
Rabbis considered to be a particularly distasteful form of
biblical hero—the military ruffian—and classes him with the
most egregious sinners in the Bible.)

Yet a half dozen other examples are brought in this listing
to show how God punishes measure for measure. Since the
hermeneutic device has been well illustrated by now, we can
turn to the other side of the coin:

> God not only punishes measure for measure, but even for good
> things it is the case that according to the measure that a person
> metes, so will it be meted out to that person. . . . For it was
> the case with Abraham that according to the measure he meted
> out was it meted out to him in return. For Abraham ran before
> the ministering angels three times, as it is said, "Abraham lifted
> up his eyes and saw three men coming to him; when he saw
> them he *ran* to greet them . . . and Abraham *hurried* to the
> tent to Sarah . . . and Abraham *ran* to the cattle and took a
> tender calf" (Genesis 18:2–7). So the Omnipresent, praised be
> He, ran three times before Abraham's offspring, as it is said,
> "God *went forth* from Sinai, *shone forth* from Seir, *arrived* from
> Mount Paran . . ." (Deuteronomy 33:2).

This midrash falls into the "close but no cigar" category. But
it should be noted how dangerously the preacher anthropo-
morphizes to make his point. If Abraham runs for God's angels, then God must run, as it were, for Abraham's offspring.
Those are the rules.

> Abraham said to those same angels, "Take a bit of water" (Gen-
> esis 18:4); so the Omnipresent, praised be He, gave Abraham's
> offspring a well in the wilderness that watered the entire Israel-

ite camp, as it is said, "The princes dug a well, the nobles of the people cut a channel" (Numbers 21:18).

Abraham said to the angels, "Rest in the shade of the tree" (Genesis 18:4); so the Omnipresent gave his offspring seven clouds of glory in the wilderness: one to the right, one to the left, one in front, one in back, one over their heads, one for the Divine Presence among them, and a pillar of cloud which preceded them. This last cloud performed the functions of killing the scorpions and serpents, burning off the thorns and thistles, leveling the hills and filling in the valleys making the way before them a veritable avenue, stretching out straight in front of them. As it is said, "The ark of God's covenant traveled before them . . . and God's cloud was upon them by day . . . and when the ark traveled Moses said, 'Arise, O Lord, and scatter Your enemies' " (Numbers 10:33–35).

Here the preacher waxes poetic, but in the concrete way only a rabbi can. The entire Army Corps of Engineers is brought on line in the form of a divine cloud to pave the way for the Israelites in the desert for forty years. That's an awful lot of roadwork in exchange for a short spell in the shade. But when God rewards measure for measure, God does so with abundance:

Abraham said to those angels, "I shall take a loaf of bread and satisfy your hunger" (Genesis 18:5). So the Omnipresent, praised be He, gave manna in the wilderness, as it is said, "The people collected it and ground it in their mills . . ." (Numbers 11:8). Just as the baby can suckle at the breast all day and it will do him no harm, so the Israelites could eat manna all day and no harm would befall them. This is what happened to those who gave it no thought. But for those who thought about it, the manna transformed in their mouth to any taste they desired. . . .

Of Abraham it is said, "Abraham accompanied them to send them on their way" (Genesis 18:16), thus the Omnipresent, praised be He, accompanied his offspring for forty years, as it is said, "For the Lord your God has blessed all the works of your hands and known your ways in this great wilderness; it is now forty years that God has been with you, you have lacked nothing" (Deuteronomy 2:7).

With these stirring words of Moses, the *Tosefta* caps its exposition on how God rewarded Abraham measure for measure by treating the Israelites well while they wandered in the wilderness of Sinai. At this point the homily jumps three generations through the patriarchy and turns to the reward Joseph garnered for his attentions to his father, Jacob.

As we enter the Joseph material, the form of the midrash has changed. The simple correspondence "So-and-so did such and such, so God repaid measure for measure" is no longer used. Instead, we enter the world of narrative rather than formulaic analogy. So let us lean back and listen to our homilist spin the tale of Joseph's bones:

Joseph gained merit by fulfilling his vow regarding his father's bones, so when he died, none other than Moses tended to him, as it is said, "Moses took Joseph's bones with him . . ." (Exodus 13:19). This teaches us that while the entire people of Israel was occupied with despoiling Egypt, Moses was engaged in this act of charity.

But if Moses had not cared for him, the Israelites would surely have cared for him in Moses' stead. That is the point of the verse, "The bones of Joseph which the Israelites took up from Egypt were buried in the town of Shechem" (Joshua 24:32).

What happened was this. When the Israelites saw that Moses

was occupied with Joseph's bones, they said, "So be it. His honor demands that the great attend to him far more so than we small ones."

And, if Moses and Israel had not cared for Joseph, surely his own offspring would have cared for him. That is the point of the rest of the verse cited above, "in the town of Shechem . . . which was given as an inheritance to the offspring of Joseph" (ibid.). But when his offspring saw both Moses and the Israelites caring for Joseph's bones they said, "So be it, his honor demands the attention of the many far more than the few of us."

So far we have seen how the storyteller harmonizes a variety of verses regarding Joseph's bones. Rather than presume that the verses in the Books of Exodus and Joshua deal with vastly differing time periods, the midrash collapses the narrative into one moment. By anachronizing so radically, a didactic point is made about the honor due to great leaders. For the Rabbis, greatness is realized on three levels of interaction. One cannot be a public figure and ignore one's relations with individuals or the needs of one's family. So when the truly great are eulogized, they are praised on all three levels. One leader attends, as an individual, to another. A family cares for the needs of one of its members. The congregation at large pays its respects to the very one to whom it looked for guidance.

Having made its point, the midrash now turns to the miraculous side of Joseph's bones. Typically, it opens with a question for which there is more than one answer:

How did Moses know where Joseph was buried? Some said that Serah, daughter of Asher, lived yet in that generation and she went and told Moses.

Here I have to interrupt and take a moment to count on my fingers. Serah, daughter of Asher, is mentioned but thrice in the Bible. In Numbers 26:46, she is mentioned in a genealogical list of the children of the tribal leader (and Joseph's brother), Asher. She is mentioned twice more (Genesis 46:17 and 1 Chronicles 7:30) as the sister of the sons of Asher. She is otherwise without personality or development in Scripture.

It is precisely this anonymity which urges the Rabbis to provide her with a character. By means of rabbinic anachronism she becomes the "wise woman" of 2 Samuel 20:16 who counsels turning the rebel Sheba ben Bichri over to King David's general, Joab, rather than see her city besieged. It is for this purpose we need to count on our fingers, for if Serah could give counsel in the days of King David and was born just as the Jews entered Egypt at the beginning of the book of Exodus she was . . . well, she was very, very old. Certainly old enough that she was around midlife when she arrived at just the right moment to tell Moses where uncle Joseph had been buried. At the time she offered that good advice she was, perhaps, as old as the four hundred years which were prophesied to Abraham (Genesis 15:13) as the length of days the Jews would endure slavery in Egypt. The midrash resumes:

> Serah told Moses, "In the River Nile is Joseph buried, for the Egyptians took rods of metal and welded them together with tin—thus did they make Joseph a watertight casket."
>
> So Moses went and stood on the banks of the River Nile and there he proclaimed, "Joseph! The hour has come that the Holy, praised be He, is redeeming Israel. Behold, God's Presence awaits you, the people Israel await you, the clouds of glory await you. If you show yourself now, well and good. If not,

our hands are clean of the vow you adjured our ancestors to take."

The Samaritan community preserves a slightly different version of this legend in their fourth-century sacred work, *Memar Marqa*. According to this text,

> When the Israelites were ready to depart from Egypt, the pillar of cloud and the pillar of fire which were to accompany them day and night during their sojourn in the wilderness actually prevented them from leaving. Moses, Aaron and all the congregation were deeply confused by this turn of events and they feared lest some sin in the community had roused God's wrath. Moses commanded the elders that each should cross-examine all the members of his tribe. When they reached the tribe of Asher, Serah came out and said that she could explain the reason for the delay. When she came before Moses she said, "You are forgetting him! Were it not for the pillar of fire and the pillar of cloud you would leave and he would remain behind in Egypt! Indeed, I remember the day he made your ancestors vow that they would take his bones along with them when they went up from Egypt."

The Samaritan source then has Serah lead Moses, Aaron and the tribe of Ephraim, Joseph's son, to the place of his burial. When his children take up Joseph's bones to bring them to the promised land, the pillar of cloud and the pillar of fire begin to lead Israel on their forty-year journey through the wilderness.

The Rabbinic storyteller of the *Tosefta* has his own drama to play out. In his version, Serah led Moses to the banks of the Nile, where Moses explained to Joseph that the conditions he imposed upon them in his vow were now to be fulfilled:

Joseph's casket floated to the surface. Moses took it and went on his way. Now, do not be surprised at this, for it says in Scripture, "It once happened that while felling trees the blade of the axe fell off of the axe-handle and sank in the water. The logger cried, 'Oh my God!' and Elisha answered him. That man of God said, 'Where did it fall,' and he showed him the place. He cut a twig, threw it into the water there and the axe-head floated" (2 Kings 6:5–6).

The storyteller here betrays his own incredulity with the material he is transmitting. He knows he's telling a tall tale. It doesn't bother him that Serah can be four hundred years old when she shows up to tell Moses the information he seeks. The prophetically wise Sibyl was well known in the hellenistic world, so Serah could qualify for that role. But it defied the imagination that a metal casket should float. This needed some verification. Typically for the Rabbis, an event that runs against the grain of knowledge of the natural sciences is not proven with any vestige of appeal to scientific method or to empirical evidence. This is far too modern a technique to have been of use. Instead the Rabbis turned, as they always did, to the Bible for an explanation of this bizarre occurrence. Sure enough, there is precedent. It is the case of Elisha and the miracle he performed which was recorded in 2 Kings. The direct connection between that instance and the case of Joseph's coffin is now explained by the *Tosefta:*

This makes sense if we but reason from the minor premise to the major premise. If metal could be made to float in the case of Elisha, who was the disciple of the prophet Elijah, who in his turn must be considered the disciple of Moses; then when Moses, who was the master of Elijah, who was the master of Elisha, wished to make the metal float, how much the more so should it be possible.

Here our Rabbi makes use of a basic principle of biblical hermeneutic, reasoning from minor to major premise. Most often, in the rabbinic community, this principle of exegesis is used to infer legal rulings, such as leniencies and strictures of Sabbath law. Here, however, it is put to service defending the legend of Joseph's floating coffin.

Later versions of this tale are also uncomfortable with a coffin that floats of its own accord. These medieval stories attribute magical actions to Moses to make the coffin rise to the surface. In one telling of the tale, Moses takes a potsherd and inscribes upon it God's four-letter name, the tetragrammaton. When he throws the shard into the Nile, the coffin floats.

In yet another version of the story, Moses takes a gold or silver tablet, much like the ones which have been discovered with magical inscriptions upon them, and incises a picture of the prophet Ezekiel's vision of God's chariot. According to the Book of Ezekiel, chapter 1, four faces were depicted there, a lion, a human, an eagle and an ox. As the story goes, Moses throws the portion with the lion on it into the Nile, and the river roars. When Moses throws in the portion with the human image on it, Joseph's bones are collected and drawn to one place. When the eagle's lot is thrown in, the casket rises. Finally, when the segment incised with a picture of an ox is thrown into the Nile, Moses takes Joseph's bones and the Exodus begins.

It seems to me that this last midrash on Joseph's bones is powered not only by medieval Jewish chariot-mysticism, which speculated on the vision of Ezekiel, but by a particularly felicitous reading of Deuteronomy 33. There, Moses blesses the tribes of Israel in his farewell speech before his death. In verse 17 he speaks of Joseph: "His firstborn ox has majesty." Our midrashist interprets this quite literally: when Moses speaks of Joseph and intones the word "ox," majesty follows and the children of Israel can be led in the Exodus by Joseph's bones.

I wrote earlier that the *Tosefta* had more than one answer to the question of how Moses knew where Joseph was buried. Let us return to that text, then, and its second answer:

> There are those who say that Joseph was buried in the Tombs of the Kings. Moses went and stood at the pyramids and shouted, "Joseph! Joseph! The hour has come that the Holy, praised be He, is redeeming Israel. God's Presence awaits you, the people Israel await you, the clouds of glory await you. If you reveal yourself, well and good. If not, our hands are clean of the vow you adjured our ancestors to take."
>
> Immediately, Joseph's casket appeared. Moses came and took it. Two caskets traveled side by side. One was the casket of holiness—the Ark of the Covenant. The other was the casket of a corpse—in which were Joseph's bones. All who passed by asked, "What is the meaning of these two caskets?"
>
> They were told, "One is the casket of holiness, the other the casket of a corpse."
>
> They were asked, "Is it possible that a casket of holiness can be near that object most unfit ritually to come in contact with anything holy—the casket of a corpse?"
>
> So they were answered, "The corpse who lies in this casket fulfilled that which was written and deposited in this casket."

With one last invocation of measure for measure, a poignant scene of Joseph's bones marching side by side with the Ark of the Covenant is drawn. Joseph, who lived centuries before the Ten Commandments were given and deposited in the Ark, is presumed by the Rabbis to have fulfilled them in every detail. So they conceive of him as Joseph the Righteous.

Because of his special merit, a juxtaposition of the holy with the unfit takes place. A great deal of rabbinic legal text is devoted to spelling out the relationships between what is fit and what is unfit. It is, in a way, the stock and trade of rabbinic knowledge. The simplest rule is this: There is nothing on earth more holy than the Ark of the Covenant. Conversely, in rabbinic parlance, the granddaddy of unfitness (if you will, unholiness) is a corpse. The two just do not belong together under any circumstance.

It is Joseph who allows the impossible to occur. Aided by the fact that in Hebrew both "casket" and "ark" are the same word, *aron,* the casket of holiness stands side by side with the casket of death. Joseph's piety, as imagined by the Rabbis, is the very fulfillment of all that the Covenant enjoins. The rule of measure for measure requires the two to be together. The merit of Joseph's bones is so great, that Moses, receiver of the Torah, attends to them. The power of his corpse and the vow he enjoined his offspring to take were sufficient for no one less than Moses to take Joseph up out of Egypt. What could be more appropriate than the two caskets marching side by side?

How did a midrash such as this arise? One can imagine, sometime in the rabbinic era, the funeral of a community leader. The casket is in the synagogue, placed before the ark where the Torah is kept. The eulogizer takes as his theme the Righteous Joseph to whom he likens his fallen colleague. As he praises the dead leader, he evokes the entire biblical world, in which the rabbinic community felt so at home. It is in just such a setting that the *Tosefta*'s tale of Joseph found its origins. Yet, whatever its origins may have been, the Rabbis' admiration of the Righteous Joseph is apparent; even in his death he achieved greatness. Joseph's bones were rewarded, measure for measure.

Chapter Eight

DYING
· · · · · · · · · · · ·

At the recent funeral of the great rabbinic leader Wolfe Kelman, his friend Rabbi Morton Leifman eulogized him with this story: When Wolfe was a small boy his family crossed the Atlantic from Europe to Canada. His father, a well-known Old World rabbi, decided after lengthy consideration to enroll him in public school to hasten his acculturation. In order to continue his Jewish education, Wolfe's father studied Talmud with his son for two hours every morning before school began. Velvel, as the boy was called, was well versed in the intricacies of talmudic dialectic and flourished under his father's attention and tutelage. Imagine his parents' surprise, then, when they were summoned to the Canadian public school to explain their son's misbehavior.

Upon their arrival at the school the teacher took them aside and explained that their son was apparently bright, but seemed bored and distracted, and that he was disrupting the class. Wolfe's father excused himself and took his son aside. "Velvel," he asked, "is it true what this teacher says about you?"

"Yes," young Wolfe confessed. "I find school very boring, it is demeaning for me to be here."

"But why?" his father inquired.

"Papa," the boy said, "every morning before school we study Talmud. When we learn together I find out about money and contracts, marriage proposals and even sexual intercourse. We learn about so many interesting things. Then I get here and they teach me stupid nursery rhymes. Why should I care if Little Bo-Peep has lost her sheep and doesn't know where to find them?"

"Ah!" said the rabbi. "Velvel, darling, you think it is not important what you do in school, but listen to your papa. I will explain why Little Bo-Peep is important—even as important as the Talmud we learn together every morning."

"You know," the rabbi explained, "that our teacher, Moses, was also a shepherd. The Midrash tells us that once he, too, lost a sheep from his flock, just like Little Bo-Peep. Moses didn't know where to find him, so he looked and looked and walked and walked until he found the sheep. And do you know, Velvel, because Moses cared so much about one sheep, the Holy One, praised be He, made Moses the shepherd of the flock of Israel. That's why we send you to public school to learn about Little Bo-Peep."

After that, Wolfe Kelman became a model student and the story became legend. How sweet to mix a midrash about Moses with Little Bo-Peep. What a take on the New World Rabbi Kelman's saintly father must have had to recognize the Good Shepherd motif buried in a nursery rhyme. How quick-witted the old man must have been to show his recalcitrant son the value of public education. And how typical of yet another rabbi to unhesitatingly adopt Moses to his own didactic purposes.

The constant use of Moses as a model for all generations is epitomized in the phrase with which Rabbi Kelman *père* referred to him: "Our teacher, Moses." In Hebrew and Yiddish, the phrase *Moshe Rabbenu,* which can also be translated as "Moses, our Rabbi," summons up the anachronistic way in which rabbinic reading of Scripture appropriates biblical characters for its own agenda. The central human figure of the Pentateuch, he to whom God spoke "face to face" (Deuteronomy 34:10), becomes the Rabbis' Rabbi. The transformation of Moses, the Egyptian-raised Hebrew of the Bible, into the urbane, hellenized Rabbi of the Midrash is a marvel of storytelling and homily.

Let us listen and observe this transformation during one particular moment of Moses' life. We will, perhaps, be able to understand how the Rabbis subvert the biblical narrative to their own needs and purposes, while at the same time they attend to difficulties in the text. In this retelling of the death of Moses, we can watch the Rabbis struggle with theodicy, the justification of God's ways in the face of apparent evil. (I always explain what the word "theodicy" means, because once when I used it in a high school class and checked at the end of the hour to make sure that the students were following me, one bright young woman explained that "theodicy" was an epic poem by Homer.) The Rabbis of old wondered why bad things happened to good people. They tried to answer that question by assigning God a role as consoler of the bereaved. Of course, they had no better way to explicate the way God's love functions, even at the moment of death, than to tell the story of God's care and compassion at the death of Moses.

To begin following this tale, let's turn back to the *Tosefta* text we studied in the last chapter. We left off there with Moses caring for Joseph's bones. The *Tosefta* continues:

Moses gained merit by caring for Joseph's bones, so he in turn
merited that none less than the Omnipresent, praised be He, care
for him; as it is said, "He buried him in the valley . . . and no
man knows his grave to this very day" (Deuteronomy 34:6).
This teaches that Moses' corpse was carried four miles by the
wings of the Divine Presence, from the inheritance of the tribe
of Reuben to that of the tribe of Gad, as Moses himself said
when blessing Gad, "The leader will be seen in his inheritance,
for there the portion of the lawgiver is hidden away, he will
come as the head of the people, for he did the righteousness of
God and enforced God's judgments among the Israelites" (Deuteronomy 33:21).

This verse of Scripture, cited to "prove" that Moses' grave
was found in the Gaddite inheritance, has been freely translated according to the rabbinic interpretation referring the
verse to Moses and his burial. Most probably, in the context
of the section of tribal blessings at the end of Deuteronomy, it
means something else entirely and refers to the leadership of
the tribe of Gad. Here, in the free-wheeling application of
scriptural verses to "prove" one thing or another, the verse is
bent to refer to Moses, our Rabbi, may he rest in peace. Such
a pious reading is certainly in keeping with the sentiments of
the *Tosefta* passage which imagines God's Presence carrying
Moses off to his secret burial place.

Truly the *Tosefta* has persisted in its notion of measure for
measure, but with a bit of a twist. In each instance the ante is
upped. Joseph cared for Jacob, so he had none less than Moses
care for him. Who could be a more impressive pallbearer than
Moses himself? The *Tosefta* answers its own silent question
with the most spectacular answer of them all. Who has sufficient credentials to bury our Rabbi, Moses? None less than
the Omnipresent, praised be He.

The ninth-century *Midrash to Proverbs* picks up this motif in its commentary on Proverbs 14:34: "Righteousness raises up a nation." The midrash comments:

> Righteousness is great, for acts of righteousness accompany those who perform them at the time they depart the world; as it is said, "Your righteousness shall march before you, the glory of God shall gather you up" (Isaiah 58:8). Rabbi Simon commented, This verse refers expressly to the death of Moses, as it is written, "He will come as the head of the people for he did the righteousness of God" (Deuteronomy 33:21).

Rabbi Simon's statement returns us once again to the end of Deuteronomy, where the blessing to Gad is interpreted as referring to the death of Moses. Of course, it is precisely at the end of Deuteronomy that Moses' biblical death scene is recorded. Before we turn to consider that brief report, note how the preceding midrash texts have all used the word "righteousness" (*tzedakah*) to link the string of biblical verses one to another. This method of equating verses by virtue of a common root word (in this case, "righteousness") was a regular method of textual hermeneutic not only among the Rabbis, but even before them among the Alexandrian Greek interpreters of Homer. Here again we have the Rabbis reading Scripture through the lenses of their own milieu and generation while concomitantly imbuing the Bible with a divine authority that makes it bear scrutiny and interpretation which no other text could endure.

To illustrate this paradox of interpretation, let us watch how the Rabbis distort the biblical account of Moses' death to teach their own points about consolation, all the while buttressing their arguments with appeals to the authority of

Scripture and constant allusion to the biblical text. As Deuteronomy 34:5–12 reports it:

> Moses, the servant of the Lord died there in the land of Moab, by the mouth [at the command?] of the Lord. He buried him in the valley . . . and no man knows his grave to this very day. Moses was one hundred and twenty at his death, his eyes had not dimmed nor his sap diminished. The Israelites wept for Moses there in the Moabite wilderness for thirty days, then the days of mourning and weeping for Moses were completed. . . . No prophet like Moses arose again in Israel whom the Lord knew face to face; in respect to all the signs and wonders which the Lord sent him to perform in the land of Egypt, before Pharaoh and all his slaves and all his land. Nor in respect to the strong hand and the great awesomeness which Moses did in the eyes of all Israel.

Here ends the Torah, the Five Books of Moses. With this remarkable report of Moses' death at the height of his strength (at the age of 120!), the Pentateuch attributed to him is closed. There will never be another like him. At the end of the Torah, in which he was a central character for three of the five books and the narrative voice of the fifth book, Moses looms larger than life. No longer like other people, he is God's unique prophet. He saw God face to face and survived, after all, to write about it.

If modern critics and ancient rabbis were distressed that this report of his death precluded the possibility of Mosaic authorship for these verses, it did not diminish the vibrancy of the finale. Here was a death worthy of the lawgiver, the author of the Torah, the man who led the Israelites from slavery unto freedom. Nowhere was the character of Moses depicted more powerfully than in these last moments of life and first moments of death.

Ponder, then, how the *Midrash to Proverbs* continues its accounting of the death of Moses:

> Rabbi Abbahu said, Come, see how hard it was when our Rabbi, Moses, had to depart the world. When the Omnipresent, praised be He, told him that his time had come to depart the world, Moses began to scream and cry. He said to the Omnipresent, praised be He, "Master of the Universe, did I labor in vain? Did I work like a horse for your children for nothing? Now is my end to be the grave? My finale to turn to dust? If you could just see it my way, from this point onwards why don't you punish me with suffering, just don't turn me over to the bonds of death."
>
> King David said of this, "O God, punish me with suffering, give me not unto death" (Psalm 118:18).

Before we turn to God's response to Moses' request, let's take a few moments to observe how very mortal Moses seems in this characterization. No longer is he the strong man of the Bible, the prophet who stands face to face with God. Here, even in the midst of conversation with the Almighty, Moses is pathetically human. He desperately bargains with God, thinking he would prefer suffering rather than death. Moses is suddenly Everyman, full of denial and avoidance. He is caught wholly unprepared for his last moments and intercedes on his own behalf as he had done so many times during his lifetime for Israel.

We will see how thoroughly this ninth-century midrashist rewrites the biblical text to conform to his own, medieval notions of dying. Compared to either biblical or early rabbinic narrations of death, the *Midrash to Proverbs* presents a surprisingly modern picture. It's as though the author has carefully read Elizabeth Kübler-Ross and adapted the biblical account to reflect her theory of stages in the process of dying. Perhaps people have not changed as much as we'd like to think they have in the last millennium, from the Middle Ages through post-Enlightenment.

God's coming response is particularly acute, for the homilist envisions a God who is omnipotent, omniscient and omnipresent. Despite God's overwhelming power, however, we will see that the midrashist depicts God as deliberately limiting the exercise of that power. This stricture of God's omnipotence is, perhaps, the weakest part of the *Midrash to Proverb's* theology and theodicy. God takes on a limited role for the sake of the ecology of the universe.

Through omniscience and omnipresence, God grants Moses' wish to suffer rather than die. As it happens, it is not the kind of suffering Moses had in mind, and God's wisdom becomes manifest. Moses realizes that his life has come to an end and prepares for death:

> The Omnipresent, praised be He, answered, "Moses, I have taken a vow that one kingship may not overlap with another by even a hairbreadth. Up until now, you have ruled over Israel, but now it is Joshua's turn to rule them."
>
> Moses responded to the Omnipresent, praised be He, "Master of the Universe, in the past I was the master and Joshua my disciple. Now, I'll be his disciple and he will be my master, just so long as I not die."
>
> The Omnipresent, praised be He, said, "If you can do this, go right ahead."

So the test is set. Moses requests suffering, but has not imagined that he himself has determined its form. God, with infinite wisdom, is prepared to allow Moses the illusion of control over his destiny. God is gracious to whom God will be gracious; there is time enough in the divine economy for Moses to learn (and teach) the lessons of mortality.

Moses' quest for immortality sets up a role reversal between himself and Joshua. Here the homilist displays his perspicacious grasp of human psychology. It is often the case, particularly with aging parents, that a role reversal such as this takes place. A formerly strong father grows physically dependent upon the child he once dandled on his knee. A shrewd and competent mother suddenly requires her daughter to balance the checkbook and pay the bills.

With this role reversal comes a recognition from the children that all is not right. A clear perception of parental decline takes place. With that perception there is anger and resentment—anger that the parent can no longer fill his or her role, resentment at the new responsibilities thrust upon the younger generation or, perhaps, upon the one sibling who has taken over the parental tasks. What does all of this psychology have to do with our retelling of Moses' death? Let's listen:

> Moses immediately went to Joshua's door and stood there protectively waiting to serve him. Moses' posture was bowed and his hands were folded so that it escaped Joshua's notice that it was our Rabbi, Moses, who was attending to him.

Here we are firmly in the late-antique world of patrons and clients. Moses acts the part of the supplicant, the client who rises early to greet, serve and offer protection to the powerful patron. Of course, the patron's protection of the client is much more powerful, which the client acknowledges by servile posture and humility. Poor Joshua, already a minor luminary in his own right and used to such attentions, does not notice the role reversal or recognize that it is Moses himself in the client's posture. We can imagine the anger and resentment this will engender, but we need the homilist to show us from what direction it flows:

> The Israelites rose early to pay their respects at Moses' door, as they were wont to do each and every day. But they didn't find him at home and asked, "Where is Moses?" They were told, "He got up early to go to Joshua's door."
>
> The Israelites went and found Joshua, who was seated, while our Rabbi, Moses, was standing in attendance upon him. They said to Joshua, "Joshua! Joshua! What's this you've done? Your master, Moses, stands in service upon you with his posture bowed and his hands folded?!"
>
> The scales fell from Joshua's eyes and he beheld our Rabbi, Moses, standing in service upon him. At that moment Joshua prostrated himself before Moses and cried. He said, "My father! My father! My master! My master! You are my father in that you raised me from the time I was very young. You are my master in that you taught me wisdom."

Here the homilist tips his hand. If it hadn't been clear that Moses is meant to function as a psychological model in loco parentis, he has Joshua feed us the correct interpretation. He tells the reader outright that Moses (like, in fact, every rabbinic figure) is meant to be considered as a parent. Moses, our Rabbi, will teach us what we wish to know about the

death of parents and how this affects their surviving children.
Let us watch his surrogate sons play out their roles:

> The sons of Aaron stood on Moses' right side and Joshua stood
> on his left. They asked him, "Our Rabbi, Moses, what is this
> you have done?"
> Moses told them, "Leave me be, for thus the Omnipresent,
> praised be He, told me, 'Do thus to Joshua that you may not
> die.' "

This is a complex scene. Moses' nephews and Joshua raise
Moses from his servile posture. They support him in a manner
that is reminiscent of the way Moses was supported by an
older generation, by Aaron and Hur, during the battle of
Amalek. That fight involved an ambush by the Amalekites
against Israel. Joshua was chosen by Moses to lead the battle
against them, but the fate of the war was determined by
Moses. "When Moses raised his hands, the Israelites gained the
upper hand; when he lowered his hands, the Amalekites
gained the upper hand" (Exodus 17:11). When Aaron and
Hur finally propped Moses up, "Joshua weakened them with
the sword" (Exodus 17:13). It was a paradigmatic victory for
the new nation.

Here, Joshua and Aaron's sons try to relive Moses' old
glories. But Moses is canny; he knows he cannot fight any
more battles. He is also disingenuous: like a conniving old
man, setting snares and traps among his children, Moses lays
the blame for his bizarre behavior at God's feet. But it was
not God who suggested that Moses serve Joshua, it was Moses
himself. There is yet some truth to Moses' statement, for had
God not been bound by a divine oath, perhaps Moses might

have merited immortality. Don't we each believe so of our own death? And because no exceptions are made to the rule of death, anger ensues:

> Rabbi Samuel ben Nahman quoted Rabbi Yohanan: At that moment, all Israel would have stoned Joshua to death had not the pillar of cloud descended and interposed between Israel and Joshua.

This pillar of cloud has been seen before, during the Exodus from Egypt. At that time, it interposed between the Israelites, pinned against the shores of the Red Sea, and the pursuing Egyptian army. "The pillar of cloud moved from before the Israelites and stood behind them. It came between the encampment of the Egyptians and the encampment of the Israelites . . . and prevented them from drawing near to one another" (Exodus 14:19–20).

Here the cloud serves a similar function. It steps between Israel and Joshua to absorb the anger directed at him. It is, after all, anger more correctly directed against God for allowing Moses to die. But the piety of the Israelites prevents them from acting out against God, or against Moses, at whom they are also angry for abandoning them. This is equally the case with children who find themselves enormously angry when a parent dies. Rather than act out against the parent (although this sometimes happens) or against God, they turn their anger toward their siblings, their spouses or themselves.

The homilist here seems to be saying, Rather than risk harming yourself or your relations with spouse or siblings, turn your anger toward God. God can absorb your anger as a pillar of cloud can absorb stones. The missiles pass through and the cloud is unharmed. Better God should bear your anger—God is omnipotent and *will* bear it. That is part of the way God can help you when a loved one dies. It's okay to be angry at God.

The denial and anger having dissipated, Moses can now come to terms with his own death. Often this takes the form of brutal recognition that one's work is complete, there is nothing left to offer:

> They said to Moses at that hour, "Conclude the Torah for us." But Moses had forgotten the traditions and did not know what to tell them. Moses faltered, then he fell on his face and said, "Master of the Universe, 'my death is preferable to my life' " (Jonah 4:3).

How ironic that Moses should quote that most reluctant of prophets, Jonah, as he finally recognizes that his work on earth is done. Jonah complained when the plant which gave him shade withered. Moses complains only when he realizes that he *cannot* complete the Torah, for to do so means to author his own death. It is a report he cannot write; others must do it for him—afterward. This recognition leads Moses to another truth: his life's work is complete—the book of his life now includes its final chapter and verse.

This faltering Moses is not simply a rabbi who is losing his memory, the most precious commodity to a master of Oral Law. Nor is he merely a prophet lamenting his inability to remember all the revelations God gave him forty-some years ago, so he can conclude the book. At this moment Moses is both of these, but much more. He is a person who has come face to face with the necessity of his death. It is a death, unlike any other in Scripture, which takes the form of a command-ment from God: "The Lord said to Moses, 'Go up upon this Mount Avarim [literally, Mountain of Passage] and look at the land that I have given to the Israelites. See it and be gathered to your people, you too, as your brother, Aaron, has been gathered' " (Numbers 27:12–13). Now, faced with the end of the Book, Moses accepts the inexorability of the com-mand:

> When the Omnipresent, praised be He, saw that Moses had come to be at peace with his own death, God tied a eulogy to him, as it is said, "Who will stand up to Me on behalf of this evil people? Who will take a stand against Me on behalf of this people who sin?" (Psalm 94:16). Who will stand up to Me when I fight with My children at the hour when they sin before Me?

How poignant a notion the homilist spins out. Moses is not only buried by God, but is given a proper funeral, eulogy and all. What does God preach at Moses' death? God laments the loss of an intercessor. God worries about Israel without Moses to look out for them. Like a parent who comes to rely on his or her spouse to check their anger and protect the kids, God worries about what the loss of Moses will mean for God. How will God have to change now that Moses is dead? This subtle recognition is a spectacular piece of theology and con-solation. When someone dies, the ecology of the universe changes. It is not just the mourner on earth who feels the irreparable loss, God feels it as well. For God, too, there must be readjustment, a whole new sense of what "normal" means. Every death requires that God mourn and heal anew. For all of this, there's no going back on God's vow:

At that time, the archangel Michael came and bowed before the Almighty. He said, "Master of the Universe, in life Moses was yours, surely he is yours in death as well."

God explained, "It is not simply the loss of Moses which makes Me offer the eulogy which I do; it is Israel I lament for. How many times did they sin before Me and Moses stood in prayer and assuaged My wrath from them, as it is said, 'God sought to destroy them, but for Moses, God's chosen one, who stood in the breach and assuaged God's wrath from destroying them' " (Psalm 106:23).

The homilist now returns his attention to Moses, reconciled to his death and taking leave of Israel. Moses has already experienced denial and anger, sought to make a deal with God and finally come to accept his death. Now he can make peace with those around him and help them prepare for the loss:

They came and told him, "The moment has come for you to depart from the world." He said to them, "Israel, my children, forgive me for all the troubles I've caused you." They responded, "Our Rabbi, Moses, you are forgiven, you are forgiven." In their turn they said to him, "Moses, forgive us for all the times we angered you." He responded, "My children, you are forgiven, you are forgiven."

The homilist here uses Moses and the Israelites to maximum didactic advantage. He knows full well from his own experience of life and death how terribly important it is to relationships to have as much closure as possible. The author of the *Midrash to Proverbs* realizes how necessary it is for the survivors to have the feeling that they had said everything they wished to, that everything was resolved, that they not have an endless string of "if onlys" to weigh them down after the death of a dear one.

He uses Moses to teach the way to resolution, by initiating a plea for forgiveness and by forgiving in turn. It is no easy task for one close to death to turn to his "children" without romanticizing the life he is leaving. With a clear head, now like the biblical Moses, he recognizes that the relationship has been stormy. Oh, how Moses troubled the people of Israel. He forced them to observe God's laws, he wrenched them from the comforts of enslavement to the responsibilities of freedom. Moses made extraordinarily difficult demands upon Israel. It would have been easy enough for Moses to rationalize that he had done it for their own good. Instead, he recognizes the cost he has imposed upon them and seeks forgiveness.

The people of Israel in their turn are no longer bitter. They, too, have come to terms with the impending death. Moses' act of contrition frees them from resentment at his departure and turns them instead to help him, psychologically, on his way. It would have been easier to continue their own denial and tell Moses, Don't worry, there's nothing to forgive you for. Instead, they catch sight of his need and forgive him, following up with their own apology. They recognize how important he was to them, and what all the anger that he evoked meant. The people of Israel realize that Moses risked alienation of their affections for the sake of making them an independent nation, a covenant people. He was a successful parent who raised his child, Israel, to maturity.

Forgiveness having been achieved, Moses now has the luxury of mourning his own death. Here he will cry, not in anger and denial, but in sadness for the loss of self:

> They came and told him, "There is but half a moment until you must depart from the world." Moses took his two hands and placed them on his heart. He cried and said, "Now it will literally happen that these two hands which received the Torah from the mouth of the Almighty will fall off in the grave."

It seems at first blush that Moses is still engaging in pathos. But the word he uses, "literally," has a technical exegetical function in midrashic literature. Moses himself is doing midrash, interpreting the last part of the Pentateuch so there can be no mistaking its intent. He will die, just like everyone else. He will be buried and his body will decompose, just like everyone else. Despite the unusual circumstances surrounding his death and burial ("No one knows where his grave is, to this very day"), one should not presume that he has left the earth, mystically, and ascended to heaven to return godlike to earth.

The midrashist captures the reticence of the scriptural account with the word "literally." He wants his readers to understand that Moses is not a god. The very ambiguity of the biblical account is meant to preclude people from turning his gravesite into a shrine. He will die like everyone else. And, as we will soon see, he will be resurrected like everyone else.

> They came and said to him, "The moment has concluded, you must depart from this world." At that, Moses uttered a great cry to the Omnipresent, praised be He. He said, "Master of the Universe, if you take my soul in this world, will you return it to me in the Future to Come?"

The Omnipresent, praised be He, reassured him, "By your life! Just as you were the head of them all in this world, so in the future you will be the head of them all in the Future to Come, as it is said, 'He will come at the head of the people' " (Deuteronomy 33:21). Why is this to be so? Because of the righteousness he performed with Israel, as it is said, "He did the righteousness of God and enforced God's judgments among the Israelites" (ibid.).

Only here at the very end of the story is the standard rabbinic invocation of resurrection of the dead mentioned. In earlier midrashim, this would have been the primary means of consolation and theodicy: all will be set right in the world to come. Yet here, our homilist waits until the promise of resurrection seems almost an afterthought. I do not think he believed any less firmly in resurrection of the dead than did his rabbinic predecessors. Rather, the author of the *Midrash to Proverbs* sees other ways of offering consolation in the here and now. He is not spelling out a systematic eschatology—what will happen in the end of days—but he is trying to expose a process that people go through in coping with death and separation. In the stages of denial, anger, striking a bargain, coming to terms and seeking forgiveness, in that march toward death lie the seeds of consolation. Our midrashist also works hard to show God's role in the process, and so offers theological consolation above and beyond the psychological.

His concern is with the dying and their survivors, not with the resurrected and their messiahs. It is for that reason that he is almost ironic when he invokes God's promise of resurrection. When Moses asks for that last consolation before dying, the promise of renewed life in the Future to Come, God responds with a vow. "By your life," God says, mirroring the human penchant for taking vows by invoking God. Yet here, Moses has just been informed that the last moment of his life has arrived. The tenuousness of the promise of resurrection could not be clearer; stronger consolations must be available in *this* life.

Here, the midrash captures the worldview of the Pentateuch, for the Torah is concerned far more with this world than with the world to come. At the same time, the rabbinic preoccupation with eternal life paradoxically turns to exegesis of Deuteronomy 33. The midrashic reading comes full circle, returning to the theme of Moses' righteous behavior and recapping the exegesis of Deuteronomy 33:21. It is this interpretation of Scripture which powers the rereading of Moses' death. The homilist prefers to infer the details of that great leader's passing from midrash on Moses' blessing of the tribe of Gad rather than read the biblical account of it one chapter later in the very last verses of the Torah.

Why should one prefer the midrash to the simple reading of the scriptural text, the *peshat*? Because it is very often the case, as here, that the lesson of the reading is more powerful than the actual words in the Book. In the case of the death of Moses, the complex of stages experienced by that great teacher, by his successor, Joshua, and by the community of Israel is fully represented in the homilist's rendering. In the actual biblical narration the emotional distance traveled by all the parties involved is obscured by the brevity of the text. Here, even though on the surface the midrash seems to represent a death-of-Moses at odds with the scriptural account, in the depth of its unfolding it captures the biblical intention almost perfectly. For who is Moses of the Pentateuch if not Moses, our teacher?

Chapter Nine

SIBLINGS
. . . .

Moses died alone, bereft of human companionship, having outlived his generation. Only God accompanied that old man to his grave, for Moses had lived long enough not only to see the promised land, but to see his friends, colleagues and family die before him. No one was left with whom he could just sit and schmooze about the taste of the onions and garlic and melons of Egypt. No one could recall with him the revelation at Mount Sinai, the plagues of Egypt and the miracles. His brother Aaron could no longer wistfully throw handfuls of dust in the air with him, as they did when they recalled bringing the plagues down on Pharaoh and his minions. Miriam his sister could no longer sing along with him, as they had together when they led the Israelites in the Song at the Sea.

It's hard, even for a Moses, to bury a big brother and big sister. He missed Miriam, who had watched out for him ever since he was a baby. Like Moses and like Aaron, she was blessed with the gift of prophecy. This gift they shared bound the siblings in a special way. When she and Moses sang together, Miriam's gift was displayed. When she sang at the crossing of the Red Sea, it was specifically identified: "Miriam the *prophet,* sister of Aaron, took the tambourine in her hand; all the women followed her, with tambourines and timbrels. Miriam led them in this song: 'Sing unto the Lord, for mighty is God's pride; drowned in the sea are the horse and its rider' " (Exodus 15:20).

The various midrashim on this verse note Miriam's status vis-à-vis her brothers. One, noting that Moses sings the same lyrics in Exodus 15:1, says that just as Moses led the men in song in gratitude to God for their deliverance, so Miriam led the women. The implication is that just as Moses was a prophet, so too, Miriam must have been equally a prophet. Another midrash, found in the Babylonian Talmud, queries the first part of the verse:

> "Miriam the prophet, sister of Aaron." Why does Scripture identify her as the sister of Aaron and not the sister of Moses? It teaches that she offered her prophecy while she was the sister of Aaron but not yet the sister of Moses. What she predicted was this: "In the future my mother will give birth to a son who will redeem Israel." When Moses was born, the entire house filled with radiance. Her father came and kissed her on the head. He said, "My daughter, your prophecy has been fulfilled." When it came to pass that they placed baby Moses in a basket on the river Nile, her father came and poked her in the head: "Well, daughter, where's your prophecy now?" So it is written, "His sister stood waiting from afar to know what would be done with him" (Exodus 2:4)—to know what would be the end of her prophecy.

The Bible makes it clear just how good a big sister Miriam was to Moses, for her watchfulness brought him to be raised in the house of Pharaoh while still being suckled by his own mother, Yocheved. But, like many big sisters, it was easier for

Miriam to be good so long as Moses played the little brother. When her prophecy came true and Moses served as God's vehicle for the redemption of Israel, her attitude became more complicated, less maternal.

Just before the incident of the spies being sent to reconnoiter the land of Canaan, Miriam and Aaron suffered an attack of jealousy toward their brother, Moses. The precipitant was his taking a wife, a Cushite woman. Maternalistic big sisters never think the women their little brothers marry are quite suitable, and so they gossip with their other siblings. Since direct reproach of the impending union is simply not done, different causes are found for complaint. Numbers 12 tells the story of Aaron and Miriam's gossip about Moses with startling frankness. It captures the spitting image of sibling rivalry:

> Miriam and Aaron gossiped about Moses because of the Cushite woman he took, for he took a Cushite woman. They said, "Does the Lord speak to Moses alone? Does God not speak to us, too?" And God heard. Now that man, Moses, was the most humble man on the face of the earth.
>
> Suddenly, the Lord spoke to Moses and to Aaron and to Miriam: "Go you three to the Tent of Assembly." So the three of them went. The Lord descended in a pillar of cloud and stood at the door of the Tent and called, "Aaron and Miriam!" So the two of them went out.
>
> God said, "Listen well to My words, if you please. If you have had prophecies from God, I have made Myself known in visions, through dreams did I speak with you. Not so My servant Moses; of all My household he is most trusted. I speak with him mouth to mouth, clearly and not in riddles. He sees God's visage. Why do you not fear to gossip about My servant, Moses?"
>
> God's wrath was kindled against them, and God went. The

cloud lifted from the tent and Miriam was leprous, white as snow! Aaron beheld her; she was leprous.

Aaron spoke to Moses: "Please, my lord, do not account against us, please, the sin that we have sinned against you. Let us not be like a stillborn child whose flesh is half eaten."

Moses cried to God, "God, please, heal her, please."

God said to Moses, "If her father spit in her face, would she not be shamed at least seven days? Let her be set apart from the camp for seven days and only afterward be gathered in." So Miriam was set apart from the camp for seven days, and the people did not travel until she was once more among them. Then the people traveled from Hatzerot and encamped in the wilderness of Paran.

Like all sibling rivalry, nothing is easy in this story. Every one comes into the narrative lugging baggage from their past; the biblical text is heavily laden with assumptions and nuance. With one early midrash on this passage as tour guide, we can reread the story and unpack it. Using the earliest commentary on the text we will also watch how the Rabbis atomize the text as they make their separate points. Yet, for all its fragmentation, the midrash will lead us back to the relationships between Moses and his siblings.

Let's start with the mystery woman from Cush. Who was she? Did Moses, like Jacob, have more than one wife? Anything's possible—we don't know much more than what we see before us. Moses' first wife was Zipporah, daughter of Jethro, a.k.a. Reuel, priest of the Midianites. We read about Moses' marriage to her in Exodus 2:16–22. She thought Moses was, by the looks of him, Egyptian (One imagines her saying, Funny, you don't look Jewish). The point here is that Moses was very dark, swarthy, easily mistaken for an Egyptian. Who were Egypt's next-door neighbors? The Cushites, who are generally identified as Ethiopians.

Did Miriam and Aaron gossip because Moses took a *black* wife? The Rabbis think quite the opposite. In the *Sifre to Numbers,* the midrash on this passage identifies her as Zipporah. She is called Cushite because even though she had aged she remained beautiful. The midrash amplifies:

> But was she a Cushite? She was Midianite. Rather, it should be understood to teach us that just as a black woman is recognized by her skin color, so Zipporah was recognized by her good deeds . . . and so it says in another scriptural passage, " 'Are you not like the inhabitants of Cush to Me, O children of Israel,' says the Lord" (Amos 9:7). Were Israelites actually Cushites? Rather, it should be understood to teach us that just as a black is recognized by his skin color, so Israel was recognized by the love the Omnipresent showed them.

Here the Rabbis take blackness as a sign of distinction and sermonize not only about Miriam, but about the distinctions of Israel as a people. I suppose if the Rabbis have a line on being a Cushite it would be that well-known quote from the 1960s, "I am black and beautiful" (Song of Songs 1:5).

After Miriam and Aaron gossip about Moses, notably complaining about his special status with God rather than mentioning his Cushite wife, the text comments (using the voice of the Omniscient Narrator par excellence), "And God heard." This statement conceals as much as it reveals. What does it mean that "God heard"? Is this a phrase associated with hearing vicious gossip? Remember back when Reuben bedded his father's concubine, Bilha, the text of Genesis 35:22 commented, "And Israel heard."

The *Sifre to Numbers* offers two comments on this verse. "God heard" teaches us that there wasn't another creature near them; Aaron and Miriam gossiped just between themselves, but *God* heard them. Rabbi Nathan links this verse with the one that follows by suggesting that they gossiped so in front of Moses! Scripture reads, "And God heard. Now that man, Moses, was the most humble man on the face of the earth." Rabbi Nathan suggests the juxtaposition of verses should yield the following: they spoke so in front of Moses but because he was so humble, he suppressed the matter. Thus it was up to God to redress Moses' grievance.

I want to continue this fragmentary exegesis. Like much of early rabbinic midrash, the *Sifre to Numbers,* edited in the third century, atomizes the verses, drawing moral lessons from each separate context. No attempt is made to string these disparate lessons into a flowing narrative. Rather, each fragment of Scripture carries its own didactic lesson. Here I will reproduce some further examples from the Miriam narrative not only to taste the flavor of early rabbinic commentary, but to show a method of atomistic analysis. It is a form of close reading that is still carried on today, often with similar moral profit.

> "God's wrath was kindled against them, and God went." Only after making clear to them what their moral failure was did God withdraw from them. We may reason from minor to major premise. If God-who-spoke-and-so-the-world-came-to-be does not display anger until God has made clear the reason for that anger, how much the more so should mere flesh and blood be at pains to make clear the reasons they are angry at another mortal.

Here the midrash moralizes using God as an example. This is typical of rabbinic exegesis, for it views the Bible as a didactic text. God's behavior is not capricious, showing beneficence in one instance, unaccountable anger in the next. Rather, the Rabbis assume, God's behavior is meant as a lesson to us all. Here, using the principle of *imitatio Dei,* we learn the proper moral code. Similar lessons could be drawn from Moses' humility. The midrash presents us with the exegetical tools to extract these lessons from the text. The inherent evil of gossip is all too obvious to the Rabbis, who elsewhere liken gossiping to murder. It is the other, more subtle, moral lessons that require exegetical virtuosity.

Since the Rabbis were part of a religiously observant community, they used the text for information on their ritual norms, as well. The *Sifre to Numbers* comments on Moses' prayer on behalf of Miriam (which totals eleven letters in the Hebrew text):

> Rabbi Eliezer's disciples asked him, "How long should a person draw out his prayers?" He answered them, "One should pray no longer than did Moses, as it is said, 'I supplicated God, as at first, for forty days and for forty nights' " (Deuteronomy 9:18).
>
> The disciples then asked him, "How brief should a person make his prayers?" He answered them, "No briefer than Moses, as it is said, 'God, please, heal her, please' " (Numbers 12:13).
>
> There's a time to draw out prayers, and there's a time to make them snappy.

I think the inferences of the *Sifre* are obvious here, though it is refreshing to see leaders of organized religion admit that sometimes a short prayer is as effective as a lengthy one. One last comment from the *Sifre* on this passage will bring us back into an orbit we have traveled before:

"Miriam was set apart from the camp for seven days, and the people did not travel until she was once more among them." This teaches that by the same measure that a person metes out, so is it meted out to that person. Miriam waited for Moses a while, as it is said, "His sister stood waiting from afar" (Exodus 2:4), therefore the Omnipresent kept God's Presence, the Ark of the Covenant, the priests, Levites, all Israel and the Seven Clouds of Glory waiting for Miriam in reward, as it is said, "The people did not travel until she was once more among them" (Numbers 12:15).

Now that sister Miriam has been returned to the camp of Israel, it would be well to note that the people benefited from her presence among them. The *Midrash to Proverbs* explains her gifts by linking her to her siblings:

"The wisest of women builds a house" (Proverbs 14:1). This refers to Yocheved, who built her house by raising three righteous persons in the world: Moses, Aaron and Miriam. Each of the three of them had the privilege of serving Israel. Each of the three of them was a benefactor of Israel. Through the merit of Moses, Israel was blessed with manna. Through the merit of Aaron, Israel was blessed with the Seven Clouds of Glory. Through the merit of Miriam, Israel was blessed with the Well which miraculously traveled through the wilderness with them wherever they wandered.

When Miriam died, the midrash reports, the well vanished, but returned to provide Israel with water through the combined merits of her brothers Aaron and Moses. When Aaron died, the clouds vanished, but returned again to guide Israel through the wilderness through the merit of Moses. When Moses died, the manna ceased to fall, the clouds dissipated and the well dried up. The gifts of these three righteous siblings stopped benefiting the people Israel only on the eve of their entry to the promised land, a land flowing with milk and honey.

All of the honey in the world cannot take away the bitter imbalance that the scriptural account renders above. It is difficult to decide whether the Torah here is male chauvinist in its treatment of the gossip against Moses or whether it is decidedly tilted to favor the Aaronide priesthood. Whichever the motivation, readers would do well to notice that though they gossiped equally, only Miriam was punished for her cruel tongue. Brother Aaron was let off the hook.

Aaron has an astonishing track record for escaping punishment. It seems as though the Bible will bend over backward to exonerate him. Modern Bible critics would probably attribute this tendency to the priestly redactors of the Pentateuch and their desire to keep pristine the reputation of their ancestor. Or perhaps it was the clouds of glory associated with his name that washed Aaron clean of the sin of gossip.

The tendency toward excusing Aaron is well founded elsewhere in the Pentateuch, most particularly in the two narratives about the Golden Calf. In the first telling of the story, in Exodus 32, Aaron is an active participant; it is he who actually forms the idol. In the retelling of the story in Deuteronomy, Aaron's role is virtually obscured. Only Deuteronomy 9:20 gives any clue that Aaron was involved in the incident of the Golden Calf, and that only by implication.

The whitewash of Aaron is picked up by the Rabbis, who have only good to say about the first priest of the people Israel. This is surprising, since there was little love lost between the academic rabbis and the dynastic priests, each group jealous of its status and power in the Jewish community. Yet, shortly after the destruction of the Jerusalem Temple, the power locus of the priesthood, the Rabbis very graciously advised their students: "Hillel used to say, 'Be among the disciples of Aaron, love peace and seek after peace. Love all creatures that you may bring them close to the Torah.' "

Although the Rabbis saw the priesthood as competitors, they respected the biblical institution even as they co-opted it. Once the Second Temple was destroyed in 70 C.E., it was much easier for the Rabbis to be generous to their vanquished competitors. They recognized, too, that the Bible was chock-full of injunctions to the priests and Levites—the clan of Moses and Aaron. We have already seen how thoroughly the Rabbis claimed Moses for themselves. To a lesser extent they did the same with Aaron. The parameters of their adoption of the priestly injunctions of the Bible are well illustrated by a story in the Babylonian Talmud. The tale draws on the very passage that was used to justify Hillel's transformation of Aaron into a peace lover. The prophet Malachi (2:5–7) has God say of the tribe of Levi, the clan of the priesthood:

> My covenant of life and peace was with him. . . . True Torah was in his mouth, no error was found on his lips, in peace and rectitude he walked with Me, many he turned away from sin. For the lips of the priest preserve knowledge; seek Torah from his mouth, for he is the angelic-messenger of the Lord of Hosts.

Let's listen as the Talmud takes this high-minded biblical rhetoric praising the priesthood and turns it into a ribald farce about the problem of finding good teachers in the local Hebrew schools:

> Once there was a certain rabbinical student who had a notorious reputation. Rav Yehuda pondered whether or not to fire him,

but they needed a teacher. On the other hand, his exploits were such that it disgraced God's Name to have him teaching. They asked the sage, Raba bar Bar Hana, "Have you any wisdom to offer on this matter?" He said, "Thus Rabbi Yohanan taught, What is the meaning of that which is written, 'For the lips of the priest preserve knowledge, seek Torah from his mouth, for he is an angelic-messenger of the Lord of Hosts'? If a teacher resembles an angelic-messenger of the Lord, then you may seek Torah from his mouth. If not, then do not seek Torah from his mouth."

Rav Yehuda fired the student. After a long while Rav Yehuda grew ill and the Rabbis came to visit him. That student came too. When Rav Yehuda saw him he began to grin. The student said, "It's not enough that you fired me, now you are going to laugh at me, too?"

Rav Yehuda replied, "I'm not laughing *at* you, I'm just delighted to be departing this world without ever having knuckled under to the likes of you." At that, Rav Yehuda expired.

The student went to the academy and asked to be reinstated. After some debate the Rabbis decided they could not reinstate the student owing to the poor reputation he continued to have. The student left the academy in tears. At that moment a wasp flew toward him, stung him on his penis and he died.

We learn three things from this story. First, the Rabbis are not afraid to appropriate verses about the priesthood and apply them to their own profession. Second, they retain a vigorous standard for the instruction of their children. One needs to have a spotless reputation to teach and to enjoy the approval of the sages. Third, we learn just what part of the student's reputation was tarnished by noting that the story, like so many others we have seen, ends with an invocation of the principle of measure for measure. As he sinned, so was he punished. In this story it was the wasp who was God's angelic-messenger, not the rabbinical student or the priest.

No matter how much the Rabbis usurped and even parodied the priestly prerogatives spelled out in the Bible, they were faced with difficult exegesis regarding the first priest, Aaron. His life contained bitter tragedy. But nowhere in the rabbinic commentaries is it suggested that his personal tragedy came to requite either his sin of gossip or the sin of the Golden Calf in typical measure-for-measure fashion. For once, this simple exegetical device fails the Rabbis in explicating Scripture. The literature is thoroughly divided on explaining how it came to pass that on the very day of Aaron's investiture as High Priest, his two sons were put to death by fire from heaven.

The puzzling death of the two siblings, Nadav and Avihu, is reported in the Bible on four separate occasions. Each time, the account differs until we are left with no clear idea of what actually happened. In fact, one is suspicious that part of what the Bible is trying to teach in recounting four versions of the episode is that there is no one correct account of tragedy. Much as Scripture itself imparts a differing message depending upon the reader and the hermeneutic approach that reader brings to the text, so the events Scripture records have no objective history beyond what the historian brings in the telling. Everything depends on one's point of view.

To put the story of the death of Aaron's sons in this light it helps us to recall how the Japanese filmmaker Akira Kurosawa experimented with point of view in his classic movie *Rashomon,* a story of a rape and murder. To paraphrase the Japanese priest who serves as the film's narrator, "It was horrible, incomprehensible. Who can understand it? War, famine, plague, wind, fire—these I can understand, but this story defies comprehension."

In the movie there is no irony as the priest makes his report. It is not at all clear what, in fact, has occurred at Rashomon. As rain pours down from the heavens, three versions of the story, then a fourth, are told. Kurosawa's experiment with point of view explains clearly how one's perspective about violence changes the very act itself. This vision offers a keen frame for the four brief reports of Aaron's anguish, the death of his sons.

Before we turn to the biblical narrations of events, let us set the scene. It is Yom Kippur, the Day of Atonement, and the rituals for achieving forgiveness for the Israelites are to be carried out by the High Priest, inaugurated that same day. Aaron has been chosen to be the High Priest, the ceremonies are set, the pageantry spelled out, the roles learned. His sons are excited—who wouldn't be—their uncle Moses is practically a king and now their father is to be High Priest and enter the Holy of Holies in the Tabernacle where God resides! Nadav and Avihu, the two elder sons, are to assist; they are princes of the tribe of Levi, future leaders of the people. Their younger brothers, Elazar and Itamar, look on in anticipation.

The biblical accounts will be offered now in the order of their appearance in Scripture. The first telling is the longest.

> Moses and Aaron came to the Tent of Assembly and went out to bless the people. The glory of the Lord was seen by all the people. Fire came from the Lord onto the altar and consumed the offering. The people saw this; they murmured and fell prostrate.

> The sons of Aaron, Nadav and Avihu, took each his fire pan, put fire therein and incense on top. They offered before the Lord strange fire which God had not commanded.
>
> Fire came from the Lord and consumed them; they died before the Lord.
>
> Moses repeated to Aaron that which God told him, "By those close to Me shall I be sanctified and before the entire people be glorified."
>
> Aaron was silent. . . . (Leviticus 9:23–10:3).

Four points are made in this narration, the first and last of them framing the actual recounting of Nadav's and Avihu's death. First, Moses and Aaron offer sacrifice, which God consumes with fire from heaven. The boys seek to emulate their elders by offering "strange fire." The Bible itself comments on the nature of this strange fire: it is that "which God had not commanded." Just as in the case of the other sacrifice, fire comes from God and consumes, but this time it is the priests and not the offering that the fire lights upon.

Moses offers Aaron what might be construed as consolation from God, "by those close to Me shall I be sanctified." This phrase is otherwise unexplained. The incident closes with the report that the father, Aaron, being installed as High Priest, continues with the sacrificial ritual. He does not protest, he does not mourn, he is perhaps dumbstruck by the events he witnessed.

The remaining three reports in the Bible are much briefer and will be offered without individual commentary:

> The Lord spoke to Moses after the death of Aaron's two sons, for they had drawn close to God and died (Leviticus 16:1).

Nadav and Avihu died before the Lord for they offered strange fire before the Lord in the wilderness of Sinai. They had no sons, and Elazar and Itamar served as priests before Aaron, their father (Numbers 3:4).

Nadav and Avihu died, for they offered strange fire before the Lord (Numbers 26:61).

I will presume, no more than did Akira Kurosawa, to decide what actually happened. There was violence; fire rained down from heaven and destroyed two lives. Like the priest at Rashomon who wishes his faith restored, the Rabbis in their midrashim to these verses seek to make sense of the reported events.

Close to half of the rabbinic commentators on these passages seize upon the notice in Leviticus 10:3, "By those close to Me shall I be sanctified." They infer from the term "close" that Nadav and Avihu were spiritually close to God, that they were wholly righteous. Because they were pure young boys without sin, somehow through their spectacular death they sanctified the altar and made it fit for animal sacrifice to God. Their very death serves, like the Yom Kippur sacrifices which their father would offer, to expiate the sin of the people Israel. Of course, it is this connection between their deaths and Yom Kippur (the portion from Leviticus 16:1 is the lectionary reading in synagogues on Yom Kippur) which leads to the midrashic conclusion that the death of these two boys serves an expiatory function. But the theology here was too close to Christian theology of the cross for the Rabbis to be very comfortable embracing it wholeheartedly. In the end, the Rabbis chose to look for the sins which were the cause of Nadav's and Avihu's death.

Still working on the text which refers to them as "those close to Me," some Rabbis suggest that the reason the Bible goes to the trouble of four discrete mentions of the event teaches us that these were the only sins the boys had committed. Explicit mention is made of the sins which besmirch what are otherwise wholly exemplary lives. But this, too, remains an unsatisfactory theodicy in light of the pyrotechnics that accompany the narrative. For the sake of expiating God's guilt in the story, the other Rabbis prefer to believe that Nadav and Avihu had sinned and richly deserved their exemplary death. In these instances, Aaron's silence was mute recognition of God's immutable justice.

My colleague in Jerusalem, Dr. Avigdor Shinan, has surveyed these stories and found an even dozen sins generally attributed to Aaron's sons. Six are ritual sins, against God. Six are moral-ethical, against fellow humans. The ritual list first:

1. "They drew near." This is mentioned as a cause in Leviticus 16. Various midrashim explain that they came too close to the altar or they came into the Holy of Holies at the wrong time (as that passage in Leviticus goes on to prohibit). All the midrashim attribute actual approach to the altar as the cause of their death. Although to us it does not appear to be a sin, the taboos of holiness associated with God's altar make this a reasonable cause of death within the biblical worldview.

2. "They offered the wrong sacrifice." This seems to be a pure invention. There is no mention of sacrifice accompanying their offering of strange fire, but might explain why they, instead of the sacrifice, were consumed by flames.

3. "They offered strange fire which the Lord did not command." This is mentioned repeatedly in Scripture. It has my vote for the most likely cause of death. But pronouncing

cause in this case is more a question of theology than autopsy, so we will press on to the other midrashic rationalizations of the tragedy.

4. "They were unwashed or ritually unfit." Here, too, the worldview of taboos associated with the sacrifice system make these possible candidates for cause, even though the biblical text nowhere alludes to them.

5. "They were wearing the wrong garments." This is not to say they came to the altar wearing Levi's (even though it was their tribe), but rather that they were not wearing the garments of priesthood which Leviticus specifically enjoins.

6. "They were drunk on the job." This is a neat inference, made by juxtaposing sections of Scripture. The first report we read of the tragedy ended at Leviticus 10:3. The next four verses detail the removal of the corpses from the altar and God's prohibition against the family's mourning. Leviticus 10:8 then commands, "Do not drink wine or alcohol." The Rabbis put two and two together to suggest a cause of death for Nadav and Avihu.

With these six suggestions we run the gamut of rabbinic opinion on the ritual causes for the tragedy. The interpersonal causes are much more creative and didactic—and much less connected to the details of the narratives.

1. "They taught Jewish law in the encampment of the Israelites." At first blush this seems to be a virtue rather than a detriment. But Jewish etiquette is very severe in this regard; it requires students to defer to the legal opinions of their masters. Since the rabbi/teacher has the last word he is, in fact, granted the right to the only word. Within a given community, one and only one rabbi is designated the legal decisor for that community. To teach Jewish law on someone else's turf is

not only an egregious breach of social standards, it is tanta-
mount to rebellion. By deciding law within the purview of
their elders, Nadav and Avihu effectively made a public statement: the legal opinions of Moses and Aaron were inferior to
their own.

This is the kind of hubris which is deserving of death, not
only in the realm of rabbinic homily, but in the world of
Greek tragedy as well. As a piece of theater it is wonderful
homily. The point of the rabbinic hierarchy and the rigidity
of the seniority system is brutally reinforced in this explanation of the death of Aaron's sons. Never mind that there is no
clue whatsoever within the biblical text to suggest such an
interpretation. One can easily conjecture (with a shudder) a
social situation which gives rise to a senior rabbi preaching
such a sermon. Pity the assistant rabbi in *that* congregation.

2. "They took no advice, even from one another." This
suggestion is actually inferred from the text of the first account quoted above. When the Bible says, "The sons of
Aaron, Nadav and Avihu, took each his fire pan," there is
room for midrash. Why does it say specifically "took *each* his
fire pan"? The word "each" appears superfluous; hence the
Rabbis infer from that extra word that each boy acted entirely on his own. They took no one's advice, not even one
another's.

This reading appears to be eisegesis, as it is not readily
apparent at a first or even second reading of the text. But it is
a clever insight about youthful zeal. It takes a certain maturity to seek the advice of others, particularly in new enter-
prises. Conversely, there is a certain immaturity in insisting
"I'll do it all myself." This insistence may be admirable (while
at the same time annoying) in a three-year-old pushing his

own stroller, but it is a form of hubris in a young priest approaching God's holy altar for the first time, on the most solemn occasion of the year. Again, it seems that these verses may have served as a quarterly pretext for a senior preacher to lecture on the evils of young whippersnappers in and about the congregation. One begins to wonder who came to hear these sermons. My bet is the average age of the congregation was well past retirement. Only they could sit through such a sermon with any feeling of satisfaction.

3. "Nadav and Avihu were impatient for Aaron and Moses to retire so they could take over." This seems to be more of the same. While it strikes a familiar chord, even in the twentieth century (perhaps especially in the twentieth century), we must recall that both Moses and Aaron essentially retired feet first. In this instance the ambitions of Nadav and Avihu are far from benign.

4. "They had no children." Yuppies to the core, Nadav and Avihu chose to live for themselves alone with no thought to the Jewish future. Procreation was a commandment in rabbinic theology, and a necessary one for a small people among the nations. The need to procreate became even more pressing in the Roman Empire, particularly once it became Christian. The survival of the Jewish people was deemed to be at stake. Hence, the choice not to have children was viewed as particularly heinous. The didactic lesson, although heavy-handed, is again clearly made for the youthful listeners in the congregation—providing they haven't run out screaming by now.

Of course, Scripture supports this reading of their sin. Numbers 3:4 specifically reports that Nadav and Avihu had no children. Hence, the Rabbis make the ready inference.

From the biblical perspective, however, the midrash is quite far from the *peshat,* or simple meaning of the verse. Since the priesthood is dynastic, within the biblical system, it is essential to have offspring to carry on the lineage. When the elder sons of Aaron die childless, that dynastic obligation devolves to the younger surviving brothers, Elazar and Itamar. Had Nadav and Avihu borne sons, then their offspring would have served in their stead. This passage biblically serves to make clear the rules of dynastic succession in the priesthood. It is no more complicated and no less important than the rules which dictated Elizabeth II's accession to the throne of England. Not being British, the Rabbis use the passage to press home another didactic point about communal structure and the obligations of the younger generation.

5. "They took no wives." This midrash is inferred from the lack of children reported above. The moral lesson is somewhat different, centering on Nadav and Avihu's haughtiness. The midrash supposes them to think, "Our uncle is a king, our father is High Priest, we are princes of the tribe of Levi—what girl is good enough for us?" For the sin of being Jewish Aaronide Princes were Nadav and Avihu felled.

6. "They feasted on God's radiance." It requires some rabbinic cultural baggage to understand why this can be construed as a sin. The idea of God's radiance is a rabbinic construct which explains the numinous nature of God's Presence. It is invoked exegetically to explain how Moses, for instance, could survive without eating for forty days and forty nights on Mount Sinai when he ascended to receive the Ten Commandments. But feeding from the radiance of God's Presence is an act of incredible intimacy between humanity and the divine. Only Moses, who saw God face to face, had a right to

enjoy it. When Nadav and Avihu drew near to the Holy of Holies and witnessed God's Presence it was bad enough. To actually feed off the radiance was more than hubris; by the rules of numinous holiness, it was fatal.

These dozen different explanations span the gamut of rabbinic perplexity about the deaths of the two brothers. In the end, all twelve exegeses together prove inadequate to explain the tragedy. One last rabbinic comment on the matter takes shelter in the cynicism of Ecclesiastes in lieu of any adequate theodicy:

> The Roman emperor Titus violated the sanctuary of the Jerusalem Temple. He entered the Holy of Holies, blasphemed God, burnt the Second Temple to the ground and returned home to Rome to celebrate a triumph where he was hailed as "Conquerer of the Barbarians."
>
> Nadav and Avihu, princes of the tribe of Levi, entered the Temple, offered a fire offering to God and were immolated. It is of this that Ecclesiastes (9:2) said, "It is all the same for the righteous and for the wicked."

In explaining the deaths of these brothers, rabbinic theodicy ultimately fails, as did the Rabbis' notion of measure for measure. Yet, even as they grapple to explain God's justice, they offer a sophisticated anthropology. In all of the instances we've seen in this chapter, the Rabbis round out biblical characterizations and offer the complementary side of the personality.

Biblical Aaron is depicted as Moses' interpreter, a secondary presence to his younger brother. Worse, the Book of Exodus indicts him as the artificer of the Golden Calf. When the Rabbis turn their narrative art to Aaron he is wholly righteous, an exemplar for their disciples of the peace-loving priest. Miriam is much flatter in Scripture; except for the incident of her leprous gossip we know very little about her. The Rabbis, typically, fill in the details of the biblical account and do so by drawing both sides of her personality. They happily gossip about the causes of her leprosy, but at the same time narrate in proud clarity the story of her prophecy and her cleverness in saving her brother Moses.

For Moses' nephews, Nadav and Avihu, we have just surveyed the range of rabbinic invention. For some the boys are wholly righteous; for others they are full of youthful offense and hubris. The total picture, afforded to us by generation after generation of midrashic collectors, however, is more balanced. Like their father, Aaron, and their aunt, Miriam, these brothers show both their good sides and their bad sides. When the midrash has finished its exegeses of pentateuchal narrative, the characters that people the Book are more fully drawn, far more complex—in short, more human.

How do the Rabbis view the anthropology of the Bible? Do they share the view imputed to Genesis, that humanity is the crown of creation? Are they more pessimistic than the summation of the creation story, when following the forming of humanity Genesis reports, "God saw all that God had done, and behold, it was very good"? Do they have a more optimistic reading of humankind than the verdict passed just ten generations later, that "the tendency of the human heart is toward evil, from earliest youth" (Genesis 8:21)?

The two examples just quoted show us that the Bible itself has varying opinions about the worth and nature of humanity. The extent to which the Rabbis follow the lead of Scripture will be explored in the next chapter. Here we bid farewell to the great sagas of the patriarchs and matriarchs and to the legends of the siblings of the clan of Levi. To learn more about the Rabbis' views of human nature, we now turn all the way back to the creation of humanity, male and female, in the image of God.

Chapter Ten

ADAM AND EVE
BACK TOGETHER AGAIN

. . . .

God was lonely. Five and a half days had been enough to create a beautiful universe, but there was no one but God to look at it and say, Hey, that's good. The animals had seemed like a fine idea at the time, but they turned out to be largely inarticulate. There was, let's face it, little satisfaction for God in the mooing and lowing of cattle. The splashing and storming of the waves was better, but still not what God had wished for. God wanted someone to talk with, someone who could respond in kind.

Even the angels turned out to be duds. Oh, they could talk all right, but all they ever seemed to say was Holy, Holy, Holy. Now what kind of conversation was that? Or, if they chose to talk in sentences, they tended to be so self-righteous and prissy. Always pointing out to God the downside of every new creation. Damn those angels. No joints in their bodies, couldn't even sit down for a cup of tea and a quiet chat. Frankly, they were, well, stupid. Not a single one of them could think of a name for any of the animals. Now God would have to have that taken care of.

So God was lonely. Lately, God had taken to speaking in the plural to assuage the loneliness. "We," said God, "Us."

When the angels, perplexed, asked God what it meant, God dismissed them with the standard reply of the grammarian: "majestic plural." They, the saps, thought God was serious, from then on calling God King, Lord, or Highness. When one of the angels, aggrandizing, referred to God as the Emperor and intimated that the angels were God's host, the royal troops, it gave God an idea:

> "Let Us make Adam in Our image, in Our likeness, that one shall rule over the fish in the sea and the birds in the sky, and over the cattle, and over all the earth, and over every single thing that moves upon the earth. So God created Adam in God's image, in the image of God was he created, male and female God created them. . . . God saw all that God had created and hey, it was *very* good" (Genesis 1:26–27, 31).

The rabbis all quoted Rabbi Simon's comment on this last verse. He discerned that God had made quite a witty pun. The verse reads, "it was very good." In Hebrew the modifier "very" is written with three letters, *mem, aleph, daleth*. If you jumble the letters you get Adam (*aleph, daleth, mem*). "It was very good," explained Rabbi Simon, means "Adam was good." God was now satisfied with creation.

This Adam creature God created was, according to the midrash, quite literally "made in God's likeness." Just as the Omnipresent filled the entire universe, so Adam filled the entire universe. This macrocosmic creature remained gigantic until it sinned; only then was it diminished in size sufficiently that it could hide from God among the trees in the Garden of Eden.

But Adam's sin is not our subject at the moment, only the enormous size of the creature:

> Rabbi Joshua, son of Rabbi Nehemiah, and Rabbi Judah, son of
> Rabbi Simon, quoted Rabbi Elazar, saying, God created Adam
> to fill the entire universe. The proof that Adam stretched from
> East to West is found in Scripture: "West to East You formed
> me, setting Your hand upon me" (Psalm 139:5). And where is
> the proof that Adam stretched from North to South? "God
> created Adam on the earth, from one end of the heavens to the
> other end of the heavens" (Deuteronomy 4:32).

By now I don't have to point out that these "proofs" have
stretched the simple meanings of the verses more than a bit.
I've translated according to the tongue-in-cheek rendering of
Psalms which Rabbi Elazar offered to prove his case. But his
point is well taken; he is genuinely puzzled by the meaning of
Genesis when it says that Adam was created in God's image
and likeness.

His literalist reading is but one of many attempts of both
ancient and modern critics to wrestle with the anthropology
offered by the Bible here. It is an odd anthropology, at that,
for it explicates humanity by invoking theology. Usually we
find it works in the other direction and God is explained by
anthropomorphism or anthropopathism. It is this reverse
stance of Genesis that is, at once, original and shocking. The
Bible here suggests that in some way humanity is akin to its
creator. The midrash takes this further and suggests that God
creates humanity out of a divine need for companionship.
This perception of God's motive for creation goes beyond
Genesis in elevating humanity in the cosmic scheme.

Even so, the same Rabbis were wary of affording humanity too much cause for hubris. So they took the same verse of
Psalms adduced above to prove Adam was macrocosmic and
employed it, in a slightly different translation, for didactic
purposes:

"Back and forward You formed me . . ." (Psalm 139:5). Rabbi Shimon ben Laqish explained, "Back" refers back to the works of the first day of creation, while "forward" refers to the very last day of creation. Thus when a person merits you may say, You preceded even the ministering angels in God's plan of creation. When a person is unworthy you may say, Even the gnat and the worm preceded you.

Rav Nahman explained the verse differently. "Back" means that humanity was created last of all the works of creation. "Forward" means humanity was punished first of all.

These requisite moral lessons having been taught, we now find the midrash of two minds about the worth of humanity. The Rabbis here have captured the ambiguities of Genesis— Adam may be the crown of creation, but it is a tarnished crown.

The segment of midrash I've been quoting concludes with one last go at the verse from Psalms. It is this reading which inspired the opening paragraphs of this chapter:

Rabbi Shmuel said, "Back" means that even when it came to offering God praises, humanity managed to come last. Thus it is written in Psalm 148, "Praised be God from the heavens," and the entire section of Psalms goes on until finally, after mentioning all the works of heaven and earth, and all of the sea and land creatures it says, "The kings of the earth and all the peoples . . . young men and maidens . . . praise the name of the Lord."

Rabbi Simlai said, Just as humanity's praises didn't come until after those of cattle, beasts and birds, so humanity's creation followed that of cattle, beasts and birds. Hence Scripture orders creation by first having God create swarming creatures from the sea, and birds and then land animals. Only after all this has been accomplished, "God said, Let Us make Adam . . ." (Genesis 1:26).

Here, the Rabbis nuance the argument somewhat. What God seeks is not an equal partner, but a companion who knows how to sing God's praises. While this view elevates humanity above all other creatures, it does so with circumspection. The midrash seems to imply that all the other creatures were quicker studies and understood from the outset that their role on earth was to offer praise to the creator. Humanity, by virtue of its very closeness to God, was a bit slow on the uptake, somewhat tardy with the adulation. Still, when the time came round, humanity got the words right and God was very pleased—at least for a while.

The constant ambiguity of Genesis is captured in another aspect of the verses cited thus far. God dismissed the "majestic plural" above as nothing more than a jest, but for the Rabbis it was no joke. They were distressed at the implications that God might not have been alone at the time of creation. This plural gave rise to gnostic speculation and to dualistic thought. Christians sometimes cited the plural as a "proof" of the Trinity. All in all, the Rabbis were not happy with "Let Us make." Even as they expressed their consternation with the verse, they redeemed some moral value from it:

Rabbi Shmuel bar Nahman quoted Rabbi Jonathan saying that when Moses was writing out the Torah, he wrote the works created on each and every day. When he got to this verse, "Let Us make Adam in Our Image, in Our likeness," he demurred. "Master of the Universe," Moses said to God, "why do you give this opportunity to the heretics to open their mouths?"

God said to him, "Write! Whoever wishes to err will find a way to err."

Then God said, "Moses, will I not bring forth both great and small ones from this Adam I created? This is the reason Scripture has the majestic plural. For if the case may be that a great

person has to seek permission of a person of lesser status he may
be tempted to say, "Why should *I* seek permission of this one
who is my inferior?" Then they can say to him, "Learn from
your Creator Who created both angels and mortals. When God
came to create Adam, God sought the advice of the ministering
angels."

Once again, we see how the Rabbis insist that God teaches
moral qualities to humanity through real or imagined biblical
actions. If God seeks advice when creating Adam, even the
greatest of the great must learn to defer, on occasion, to his
lessers.

This motif is spun out by the Rabbis in a series of answers
to the question, Who *was* God speaking to when God said,
"Let Us"? All the while that the Rabbis seek to find a theo-
logically acceptable way to explain the plurals in that verse of
Scripture, they have a playful sense of satire. It was common-
place for the Rabbis to speak of God through analogy, most
often referred to as parable. The most frequent type of parable
the Rabbis employed for this speculation about God came
from their everyday life and focused on that most august of
humans, the emperor.

While the Rabbis reluctantly chose the Roman Princeps,
the First Among Equals of the Empire, as their model for the
most powerful human on earth, they had very little illusion
about the adequacies of a Roman emperor as a stand-in for
the King of the King of Kings, the Holy, praised be He. At
the same time, there was much to be gained by using the
image of the emperor for theological purposes. It never hurt
to flatter the imperium—the Rabbis were as aware of this as
anyone else who lived in late antiquity. And, if your flattery
was subtle enough, those congregants who heard it got your

point—beneath the flattery was a pointed barb at the pretensions of the emperors. This barb was particularly honed as the years went on and the pagan emperors declared themselves gods in their own lifetimes. Few emperors had any humor about this apotheosis, they genuinely believed they belonged in the Pantheon. Had he not been responsible for the destruction of Jerusalem in the war of 66–70 c.e., the Rabbis would have heartily approved of the irony of that old soldier turned emperor, Vespasian, who when dying drolly quipped, "I can feel myself turning into a god."

With this as background, we are prepared to listen as the Rabbis discuss "Let Us":

> With whom did God take counsel when God said, "Let Us make Adam"? Rabbi Joshua said, God took counsel with the works of heaven and earth. This may be likened to an emperor who had two consuls and wouldn't do a thing without their consent.

In fact, every emperor of Rome had two consuls, for the institution of two annual consuls antedates the empire. All the way back in the days of the Roman Republic two consuls were named each year to run the meetings of the Roman Senate. These consuls held both prestige and power. But with the advent of the empire and an autocratic emperor, the role of the consuls changed. Like the senate over which they presided, the consuls were now to rubber-stamp the desires of the emperor. Often, the emperor named himself one of the consuls for the year. One emperor, to show his disdain for the Roman senate, even named his horse as consul! It is, then, with a delicious sense of irony that Rabbi Joshua, keeping a straight face as he does it, suggests that God sought the advice of the consuls when Scripture reported "Us." As the works of heaven and earth were to God, the consuls were wholly creations of the emperor. It was a consultation in name only—a realpolitik form of majestic plural:

> Rabbi Shmuel bar Nahman said, God took counsel with the works of each day of creation. This may be likened to an emperor who had a co-regent and wouldn't do a thing without his consent.

Rabbi Shmuel lived in the early fourth century, at a time when the institution of co-regents was becoming regularized. The stability of the empire depended not upon equality of the two co-regents, but upon a decidedly obvious dependence of one upon the other. Usually the emperor held control of the Roman army, and with that, all the real power of the empire. True, a great show was made of seeking the advice of the co-regent, but no one was fooled. Everyone in the empire knew where the real power lay—their lives depended on it.

In taking the examples of consuls and co-regents these Rabbis ran a bit of a risk of insulting the imperium. But they relied first on their own insignificance and trusted that their comments would not be noticed. They then relied on their ability to turn an analogy between God and the regent into unabashed flattery for the purportedly insulted party.

There was a great deal to be gained from their risk. The verse could be explained in terms of an everyday situation which, though subtle, was instinctively understood by all. And the dualistic and polytheistic theologies of Christianity, gnosticism and various forms of paganism could be put into what the Rabbis saw as true perspective—their own. Yes, various groups may invoke Genesis to "prove" that God was associated with other creator-figures. But in reality these figures had no more power than did the associates of the emperor. The Rabbis distinguished sharply between form and reality and came down firmly on the side of concrete reality. There was no reality more concrete to their perception than the workings of God in the universe.

One last comment needs to be offered in this series. It is from a contemporary of the Rabbis quoted above, but one who believes in calling a spade a spade, let the niceties of diplomacy be dashed:

> Rabbi Hila said, There is no consultation here at all. This may be likened to an emperor who was strolling with his retinue in front of his palace. He saw a slab of uncut marble lying there and asked, "What shall we do with this?" Certain of his toadies suggested that he erect public baths. Others suggested that he erect private baths for personal use. The emperor finally said, "I shall make a life-size statue of myself." Who would dare contradict him?

Rabbi Hila rather brutally describes the situation, but makes his point nonetheless. God takes advice from no one. God does as God pleases. When God wishes to create something in God's image and likeness, can anyone contradict that will? This, then, was the challenge implicit when God said, "Let Us make Adam."

The Rabbis saw the downside of their own creation, for if humanity was in God's image, they expected at least that God would hew to the same standard of justice the Torah demanded of them. They preferred to think of God as perfect, but how could such imperfect vessels reflect the likeness of their creator? Was there not a great risk in the theology implicit behind such an assumption? Some Rabbis wondered if it were not better to carefully break the close nexus between God and Adam, lest errors be made about the essential nature of Creator and creature.

The Rabbis knew only too well the folk adage about the emperor, which they quoted in its original Greek (painstakingly transliterating it into the Hebrew alphabet so all could sound it out): *Para basileus ho nomos agraphos*—The law is unwritten for the king. They rejected this standard for a much higher expectation: for the King of the King of Kings there must be absolute justice; the observance of the law was paramount. In viewing God so, the Rabbis of course betrayed their own fierce loyalty to the absolute necessity of the rule of law.

And yet the text of Genesis stood before them, challenging generation after generation to set their sights high, raise their standards and attempt to fulfill the expectation that they were made in the likeness of their Creator. Fully aware of their sinful natures, they imagined God wrestling with justice in order to complete the task of creation:

Rabbi Berechiah said, When God set about to create Adam God foresaw that both righteous and evildoers would descend from him. God pondered, "If I create him, there will be evildoers, yet if I do not create him, how will there ever be righteous people in the world?" What did the Holy, praised be He, do? God ignored the image of evildoers and relied on the attribute of mercy to join in the creation of humanity. Thus it is written, "For God knows the ways of the righteous, and the ways of the evildoers God destroys" (Psalm 1:6), which is to say God destroys their ways from the realm of God's attention and joins with the attribute of mercy to create humanity.

Here the tension is acutely expressed between two conflicting attributes of God: justice and mercy. In order to create sinful humanity, a pale reflection of the perfect creator, God actually does away with justice for the moment and relies on mercy to complete the creation. The theology is astounding —it is as though God pulls a fast one in order to create humanity.

Other Rabbis characterize the theological-anthropological dilemma in different terms. Rather than work out the conflict among God's competing attributes, they ascribe these functions to angels, which are but hypostatizations of God's attributes—concrete representations of the ideas mentioned by Rabbi Berechiah above.

Rabbi Haninah said it otherwise. When God came to create Adam, God took counsel with the ministering angels. God said to them, "Shall We make Adam in Our image?"

They asked God, "This Adam, what is its nature?"

God replied, "Righteous ones shall descend from him." Thus it is written, "For God knows the ways of the righteous" (Psalm 1:6)—God made known the way of the righteous to the ministering angels. "And the ways of the evildoers God destroys"— that God kept from them. God revealed to the angels that the righteous would arise from Adam but did not reveal to them that evildoers would arise from him. For had God revealed to the angels that evildoers would arise from Adam, the attribute of justice would not have allowed God to create humanity.

Here the Rabbis state the quandary in its extreme form. God's very attributes seem to have veto power over God's will. If God is to hew to stern justice, then humanity cannot be created. So God deceives justice in order that mercy may prevail! This is, of course, wholly untenable. It proves unmistakably that nothing could be more alien to the Rabbis than the systematic pursuit of theology. What worries them here is *not* so much God's quandary and the theological paradox they have created by formulating their question in quite this way. What worries the Rabbis is the anthropology of the situation. How *can* humanity be created in the likeness and image of God if there is the possibility of sin?

The conundrum is expressed even more urgently in a midrash which immediately follows the one just quoted from *Genesis Rabbah*. There the angels are even more active in taking sides over the ambiguous nature of humanity:

> Rabbi Simon said, When the Holy, praised be He, came to create Adam, the angels formed camps and cliques. Some said, "Create!" Others said, "Don't create!"
>
> Thus is it written, "Love and truth grappled, righteousness and peace did battle" (Psalm 85:11).

Before we go on to describe the debate between the camps of angels, let's see how once again our Rabbis have played fast and loose with the text of Scripture. The translation above is an accurate reflection of how Rabbi Simon read the Psalm which shapes his homily, but it is translated in context thus: "Love and truth embraced, righteousness and peace kissed." Perhaps there is sometimes little difference between an embrace and grappling or between a battle and a kiss. But Rabbi Simon is not here to tell Henny Youngman jokes, he is bending Scripture to make a point about the dilemma of humanity created in the image of God.

> Love said, "Create humanity, for it shall perform deeds of loving kindness."

> Truth said, "Do not create humanity, for it is full of lies."
>
> Righteousness said, "Create humanity, for works of righteousness are its realm."
>
> Peace said, "Do not create humanity, for it is full of discord."

Here, rabbinic recognition of the ambiguities of human nature are played out more fully than anywhere else. The Rabbis were generally optimists who believed in the essential goodness of humanity, precisely because Adam was created in God's image and likeness. But at the moment of confronting the verse, the Rabbis recognize how terribly complicated human nature really is. In explicating the arguments of the angels and God's subsequent behavior, they give those ambiguities eloquent voice.

> What did the Holy, praised be He, do? God took Truth and flung her down to the ground. Thus is it written, "Truth is sent to the earth" (Daniel 8:12). The ministering angels protested to God, "Master of the Universe, why do you demean your most worthy platoon, Truth? Let Truth arise from the ground!" Thus is it written, "May Truth spring forth from the earth" (Psalm 85:12).

The problem now having been graphically spelled out, the Rabbis can revert to exegesis to "solve" the difficulty raised by the knotty term "Let Us." As is often the case, their solution is technical, here devolving on a pun—a repointing of the consonants of the Hebrew word for "Let Us," *na'aseh*. But while the clever Rabbis offer new vowels to solve the crux, they keep within the confines of the narrative world they

have created, thus offering a rather elegant solution to the
debate among the angels:

> Rav Huna the elder of Sepphoris said, While the ministering
> angels were arguing with one another and debating among
> themselves, the Holy, praised be He, created Adam. Finally,
> God said to them, "What are you arguing about, Adam is
> already created" (na'asah).

The simple change in the verb from na'aseh to na'asah makes
the scriptural text mean something very different. No longer
is it "Let Us make Adam"; now it is "Adam is already made."
There is no longer any problem of a plural or any question to
whom God is speaking. There is no consultation at all. Much
like Rabbi Hila's perception of God (and not without a certain reflection on that creature made in God's image), God
does what God damn well pleases—to hell with the angels
and their advice!

The Rabbis recognized yet another drawback in the verse
which asserts that humanity was created in God's image and
likeness. As we saw above, there were sages who took this
quite literally and understood Adam to be macrocosmic. It
was only natural then that a certain confusion should arise
about who was creature and who Creator. In everyday life,
the Rabbis saw this confusion manifested in the deification of
human emperors and to a certain extent, they probably perceived this to be the chief difficulty they had with Christianity. There had to be a distinction between the Creator of the
universe and Adam, whether first or last.

Again, the Rabbis use the angels as their vehicle for spelling out the problem. In attributing the error of confusion to

them, the Rabbis are also able to explain another very difficult problem in the Genesis creation narrative—a second version of the creation of humanity. Here the problem of the
first story ("in Our image, in Our likeness," Genesis 1:26–27)
is solved by the story of the creation of man and woman
related in Genesis 2:

> Rabbi Hoshaya said, When the Holy, praised be He, created
> Adam in God's image, the ministering angels were confused and
> sought in error to say, "Holy, Holy, Holy" to Adam. What
> does this matter resemble? It's like the advent of the emperor,
> when he and the governor ride together in the royal chariot.
> The townfolk all come out to see the emperor and want to
> shout *domine,* only they don't know which one is the emperor
> and who merely the local governor. How does the emperor
> solve the problem? Simple, he shoves the governor out of the
> chariot and then everyone knows who the emperor is.
>
> So, when the Holy, praised be He, created Adam, and the
> ministering angels erred, what did God do? He threw a deep
> sleep upon Adam and everyone knew who was who. Thus is it
> written, "The Lord God caused a deep sleep to fall upon Adam,
> and he slept . . ." (Genesis 2:21).

Another version of the confusion between creature and Creator focuses on yet a different verse in the second account of
the creation of humanity. Here, the ninth-century midrash
Pirke Rabbi Eliezer has God worry out the problem:

> Adam was strolling in the Garden of Eden, like one of the
> ministering angels. The Holy, praised be He, said, "I am alone
> in My universe and that one is alone in his world. I do not have
> intercourse, and that one does not have intercourse. In the end
> the other creatures will reason that since that one does not have

intercourse, it was he who was their creator. 'It is not good for Adam to be alone, I will make him a fitting mate' (Genesis 2:18)."

These two texts share a common concern about confusion between God and Adam. While the first focuses on the error of the angels, the second focuses on the potential for error among the animals. Each is essentially solved by an appeal to the process which brought forth woman. Perhaps it would help if we paused to read the Genesis account of that creation:

> The Lord God said, "It is not good for Adam to be alone; I will make him a fitting mate." The Lord God created all of the animals of the field from the ground and all of the birds of the sky and brought them to Adam to see what he would call them. Whatever name Adam gave to an animal is its name. So Adam gave names to all the beasts and all the birds in the sky and all the animals of the field, but Adam did not find a fitting mate. So the Lord God caused a deep sleep to fall upon Adam and he slept. God took one of the ribs from his side then closed the flesh there. The Lord God built up that rib from the side which God took from Adam into a woman and brought her to Adam. Adam said, "This is the one! Bone of my bones and flesh of my flesh. This one shall be called wo*man* for from *man* was she taken. It is for this reason that a man leaves his mother and father and cleaves to his woman, that they may be one flesh" (Genesis 2:18–25).

There are many points to be gleaned from this long second telling. First, we see that God, appreciating what it means to be lonely, creates a fitting partner for Adam. Although Adam did not turn out to be the partner God had hoped for, he at least solved the problem of naming the animals for God. Along the way, Adam earned a partner for himself.

But look closely and see how this account of creation contradicts the account found in Genesis 1. Here, woman is taken from Adam's rib. There, male and female are created at one fell swoop, both in God's image. I took care in this chapter to refer to the Adam of Genesis 1 as Adam, not as "he," for Adam seems to be both male and female. My colleague Phyllis Trible captures the pun in the name "Adam" and translates the word as "earthperson," since Adam was formed from the earth (Hebrew: *adamah*).

Further, I took care in my discussion, often at the expense of the elegance of the English language, not to refer to God as "He." The reason for this care also lies in the Genesis 1 account of creation, which considers God's image to be both male and female. To use gender terminology is to do a disservice to our image of God.

In the Genesis 2 account, man and woman are separate entities, man created from the dust of the earth (Genesis 2:7), woman from the rib in his side. Thus occurs a sense of ordering which places males earlier, if not necessarily higher than females. The Rabbis were then faced with a double problem. There was the question of the equality of the sexes, a question as pertinent then as it is today. Second, the Rabbis hated contradictions in Scripture and sought to resolve them whenever possible. *Genesis Rabbah* offers two approaches to these problems:

Rabbi Jeremiah ben Elazar said, When the Holy, praised be He, created Adam, God created Adam androgynously. Thus is it written, "This is the book of the genealogy of Adam, for on the day which God created Adam, God made him in God's image. Male and female God created them, and blessed them, and called their name Adam, on the day of their creation" (Genesis 5:1–2).

Rabbi Jeremiah resolves the problem of the Genesis 1 account versus the Genesis 2 account by bringing yet a third set of verses, from Genesis 5, to tilt the balance. This use of a third set of verses to resolve an apparent internal contradiction of Scripture is an old hermeneutic method of the Rabbis.

The end result here is an Adam created *both* male and female in God's image. Rabbi Jeremiah reasons that Adam was androgynous, that is, having male and female sexual characteristics, just as God must have had the aspects of both masculinity and femininity. This latter aspect, God's feminine qualities, is aptly captured in one of the epithets the Rabbis use for God, which has often been quoted in the pages of this book: God's Presence. In Hebrew, God's Presence is *shekhinah,* which is not only a feminine noun in the gender-bound language, but is treated as feminine in rabbinic appreciations of God's nature.

The midrash offers a second hermeneutic approach to the dual problem. I've given a clue to the method in my own translation of Genesis 2, above, where I refer to the rib-in-Adam's-side. It is a long-winded way of saying rib, but the following midrash will show how the linguistic nuances of the Hebrew term *tzela* can be used to harmonize the contradiction and so solve both problems:

Rabbi Shmuel bar Nahman said, When the Holy, praised be He, created Adam, the creature was two-faced. God sawed it in half, one side here, the other side there. Thus is it written, "Back and forward You created me, then You set your hand upon me" (Psalm 139:5).

His listeners objected, saying, But here it is written, "God took one of his ribs from his side" (Genesis 2:21).

He explained to them, The word *tzela͑* in that verse means his two sides, just as it means "side" in the verse "And of the side (*tzela͑*) of the tabernacle" (Exodus 26:20).

Here we see the reason that Rabbi Shmuel bar Nahman was famous as an exegete of Scripture. He returns to exegesis of the verse of Psalm 139, which we saw applied to the creation in a variety of ways above. But his real magic is saved for Adam's troublesome rib. *Tzela͑* means both "rib" and "side" so Rabbi Shmuel reads the Genesis 2 account to be the same as Genesis 1! In both accounts, according to his midrash, Adam and Eve were created together—back to back. There is no contradiction in the verses of the Torah, and male and female are partners in God's creation of them, both equally reflecting the image of their Creator.

The implication for sexuality in this view of creation is godlike. The original creature was a mingling of the sexes, and all sexual intercourse is an attempt to return to that pristine state of being—"that they may be one flesh." Other Rabbis, who observed that humans were not the only creatures who engaged in intercourse, saw sex as less a heavenly characteristic and more an earthly one. Even so, humanity held a special role somewhere between heaven and earth:

Rabbi Elazar said, God created humanity with four characteristics from Above and four from Below. From below: humanity eats and drinks as do the animals, procreates as do the animals, defecates as do the animals, and dies as do the animals. From above: humanity stands erect as do the angels, speaks as do the angels, understands as do the angels, and sees as do the angels. But don't animals see? Yes, but humans have stereoscopic vision.

So this creature God made has aspects of the angelic and aspects of the beastly. As always, the rabbinic midrash captures the mood of Scripture in its own idiom. Genesis, in all three accounts of creation (chapters 1, 2, and 5) displays a marked ambiguity about the nature of humanity. The Rabbis echo that ambiguity in their various midrashim, coming down now on one side, now on the other, to create a wholly balanced anthropology.

One last midrash to close this chapter returns to the question, Who *was* God speaking to when God said, "Let Us make Adam"?

> Rabbi Ammi said, God took counsel with God's own heart. This may be likened to a king who built a palace and used an architect for the project. When the king saw the palace and was not pleased with it, to whom did he complain? To the architect, of course. Thus it says in Scripture, "God was sorry to have created Adam on the earth, God was troubled at heart" (Genesis 6:6).

This invocation of the decision to flood the world and destroy humanity in the generation of Noah is a most poignant summary of God's dilemma. At the very moment when God decides to create humanity, God shows awareness of their coming failure. The analogy to the architect serves as an almost artificial link to carry the midrash along. Even so, as we will see in the next chapter, the idea of the architecture of the universe held a firm grip on the rabbinic imagination. It was an essential trope in their discussions of cosmology.

Regarding rabbinic anthropology, however, Rabbi Ammi drives the point home mercilessly. Humanity may be a creation which pleased God and was deemed "very good." But not for long. Only ten generations later God will regret the decision to seek companionship in humanity. God's loneliness, however, will endure for eternity.

Chapter Eleven

THE ARCHITECTURE
OF THE UNIVERSE

· ·

The first word of the Bible has an error of grammar. As the medieval authorities record it, and as seemingly all the ancient translations and midrashim attest, the Book of Genesis opens with a very knotty passage. In order to interpret it intelligently, we need to be reminded a bit about how Hebrew works. Earlier we mentioned the fact that while Hebrew has what we call consonants, essentially no vowels are written in a text. Of course, a word consisting only of consonants can't be pronounced, so vowels were added to help pronunciation. In addition, in the Semitic languages, changing the vowel can change the grammar and so, the meaning of a word. So there is a long-standing oral tradition about the proper voweling of any given word of Hebrew Scripture, just as there is an ancient tradition about where one sentence ends and the next begins, where the commas go, and so on. Much of this tradition of vowel pointing was written down in the Middle Ages, but by then our particular grammatical boo-boo had been an old and well-known crux for interpreters.

According to the vowel points which could accompany the first word of Scripture, the verses following might mean one of two things. The text could mean either "In the beginning God created the heaven and the earth" (Hebrew: *baresheet bara*) or "When God began to create the heaven and the earth" (Hebrew: *beresheet bro*). As it stands in every pointed Hebrew text, the words read *beresheet bara,* which we should translate literally as some hybrid of the two possibilities, such as "When the beginning God created. . . ."

Obviously such a translation will never do, for while it captures faithfully the dilemma of the Hebrew grammar, it makes no sense. Ever since the first translation of Genesis was made into Greek some 2,300 years ago, almost every translator has opted for "In the beginning. . . ." Only recently in this century has the "When God began to create . . ." option been offered as an alternative translation. But the difference between the two translations is more than simply a matter of style. How one irons out the wrinkle of the grammatical error determines one's theology and cosmology. Let's study the two translations and explore their different implications.

"In the beginning" presumes that God existed before matter, before time, before the big bang, before the universe. Reading that "God created the heaven and the earth" gets the show on the road. Even though it is not at all clear that this is the literal intention of the biblical narrative, early translators and the Rabbis and Church Fathers were, nevertheless, quite happy to read Genesis that way. This reading made God into the creator who brought forth a universe *ex nihilo,* out of naught. It pleased these religious authorities to define the God of Genesis as the creator of the universe who could bring forth somethingness from nothingness. A God who could create *ex nihilo* was a god worth reckoning with, especially by hellenistic views of cosmology. So, when the God of Genesis could be a creator *ex nihilo,* everybody was satisfied with the solution to the awkward grammatical slip.

The other possibility—"When God began to create"—still has to be reckoned with, if only because it may be the correct reading. Already in the eleventh century, the pentateuchal commentator par excellence, Rabbi Solomon ben Isaac, or Rashi, pointed to the veracity of this reading. If we read *beresheet bro,* the meaning of our text is quite different. The phrasing requires that we read the first verses of Scripture as a group, something like this:

> When God began to create the heaven and the earth, the earth was as yet chaotic with darkness covering the depths and mighty winds blowing across the waters. Then God said, "Let there be light," so there was light.

Here the first things created are not heaven and earth, for they already exist, though in a chaotic state. Instead, God begins creation with light—perhaps a more pleasing cosmology to the Stephen Hawkings of this world. But, pleasing or not, God's role here is profoundly different, and our theology has to be adjusted accordingly. God no longer is creator *ex nihilo;* indeed, there seems to be preexistent matter. God does bring certain elements, such as light, into being, but God mostly orders the universe into harmony and out of chaos. Given the varying cosmologies available to the scientific minds of the rabbinic era, this reading should have been reasonable enough for the rabbis to be comfortable with it as an alternative to "In the beginning. . . ."

But the rabbis were decidedly uncomfortable with "When God began." It's all the more astonishing because certain outside factors might have tilted them toward this reading. As mentioned above, the Greek translation of Scripture, the Septuagint, had long before opted for "In the beginning." By the late fourth century, that translation had become sufficiently identified with the Church that the rabbis ruefully referred to the day the translation was made as being as bad for the Jews "as the day the Golden Calf was made." Further, the Church had openly trumpeted its preference for the "In the beginning" translation when the author of the Gospel of John opened the prologue to his gospel with those very words. Since that Gospel also locates Christ "in the beginning," we might have expected the sages to flee from that rendering and point the vowels of their Scripture to read clearly "When God began to create. . . ."

Why, then, did the Rabbis, too, opt for all the difficulties associated with "In the beginning"? Well, their theology demanded that God be the creator *ex nihilo*. Another part of the reason they wanted God to be so defined may well have been a way of dismissing Christian claims for Christ's godhood. I suppose the rabbinic argument would have gone something like this: God by definition creates *ex nihilo*, out of nothing. After all, Genesis tells us that's how the world was created (the Rabbis would have serenely ignored the circular nature of this reasoning). What did this Christ guy ever create? Or, in the words of the ninth-century *Pirke Rabbi Eliezer:*

> The northern quadrant of the world is where snow and hail and extremes of temperature come into the world. Another opinion: the northern quadrant was created incomplete. God said, "Anyone who claims to be a god, let him come and finish creating this quadrant I've left. Then everyone will know whether or not he's truly a god."

Admittedly, we cannot be sure of the extent to which rabbinic fears of Christianity motivated their choice of readings. After all, the "In the beginning" tradition was in place well before Christianity captured the Roman Empire in the early fourth century. But there was another religious tradition, Gnosticism, which may also have been responsible for motivating the rabbinic preference for the "In the beginning" option. This tradition is closely associated with Christianity, particularly from the second century onward, but most scholars today see it as a pre-Christian phenomenon. Its way of looking at the world was anathema to the Rabbis, as well as what they perceived to be its dualistic theology.

Gnosticism took many forms, but among its basic myths was the assumption that the god who created the world, called the demiurge, was a lesser god and not the supreme god in the Godhead. Further, many of the Gnostic texts make clear that the demiurge fools the inhabitants of the world into thinking that it *is* the supreme god and worthy of fealty and worship. Hence the Gnostic (one who learns the special "knowledge" this religion has to offer its initiates) can learn how to awake from the slumber induced by the demiurge and find salvation through the true god.

What made Gnosticism in its various forms appealing was the theodicy or explanation of evil it offered its adherents. Did the world seem to be a lousy place? Yes, answers the Gnostic, it *is* a lousy place. We are here under the thrall of the demiurge, being deceived. Furthermore—and here's where Gnostic myth becomes relevant to our textual problem—the demiurge created the universe out of bad materials. No wonder the world stinks, the very stuff it was made from was faulty. The preexistent matter was evil, so the universe is evil.

The Rabbis, who were far more optimistic about the beneficence of God and about God's good intentions in creating the universe, rejected this argument. They also emphatically denied the dualism implicit in the Gnostic myth which posited a creator God different from the supreme God of existence. For the Rabbis, both the universe and its salvation were in the hands of the One and Only God. To hear them address the problem of preexistent matter implicit in the "When God began to create" interpretation of the opening verse of Genesis makes clear the virulence of their anti-Gnostic polemic:

> A certain ascetic monk challenged Rabban Gamaliel: "Your God is a great artisan, but look at the materials he had there to assist him: chaos, confusion, darkness, wind, water and the deep" (cf. Genesis 1:1–2).
>
> Gamaliel responded, "Drop dead! For every one of those items you suggest to be preexistent, Scripture writes that it was created. Of chaos and confusion it says, 'God makes peace and creates evil' (Isaiah 45:7); of darkness it says, 'God brings light into being and creates darkness' (ibid.); of water it says, 'The uppermost heavens and the waters praise God,' and whyso? 'For He commanded and so were they created' (Psalm 148:4); of wind it says, 'For God brings mountains into being and creates the winds' (Amos 4:13); and of the deep it says, 'The deep was formed out of nothingness'!" (Proverbs 8:24).

Gamaliel responds to his ascetic monk cum "philosopher" by "proving" biblically that everything was indeed created by God and not preexistent. It is clear from the proof-texts that Gamaliel takes the preexistent matter to be thought of as somehow evil; this is particularly noticeable in his proof for chaos and confusion from Isaiah. But the last of the proofs is the most slippery and merits a closer look, for the simple contextual meaning of that verse offers a very different translation of the Hebrew from Gamaliel's reading of it. One must admire Gamaliel's midrash, for he has twisted a passage of

Scripture into testimony that God creates *ex nihilo*—"the deep was formed out of nothingness."

If we open the Book of Proverbs to the chapter in which this verse is found we will see that Wisdom speaks there and tells us, "God created me the beginning of his ways, before the works of old. I was eternally at the head, before the oldest things on earth. *When there was as yet no deep was I formed,* when there were as yet no springs of mighty waters" (Proverbs 8:22–24). The passage I've emphasized is the same passage Gamaliel cited above, but here, translated in context, it means something very different.

And yet, in some way Gamaliel's translation attests to the rabbinic solution to the Gnostic claim of preexistent matter. Proverbs proclaims that there *was* something which preexisted creation: Wisdom. And for the Rabbis, Wisdom is wholly good, not the evil stuff of Gnostic creation stories. Not only that, but for the Rabbis, Wisdom is virtually synonymous with Torah, they are one and the same character. Because of this deep identification of Torah with Wisdom, the Rabbis happily cite these passages from Proverbs 8 to show that if anything preexisted, it was the Torah which was "first of God's ways." Here is the Rabbis' unique and startling contribution to cosmology: Torah preexists the universe.

What is even more delightful is how the Rabbis use this "fact" to unravel the grammatical difficulty in the very first word of the Torah itself. In the earliest rabbinic midrash on the Book of Genesis, compiled in Palestine in the fifth or sixth century, a great deal of attention is paid to the opening of Genesis. In fact, more than a dozen different sets of explanations seek to unknot the difficulties in the grammar of the first word. In typical rabbinic fashion, the problem of consonants and vowels is never addressed directly, but all the solutions worry through that crux.

Some of the midrashim even go so far as to treat the first letter of the first word of the Torah separately, for it is there that the awkward vowel point lies. Other exegeses divide the first word of the Torah in half, as though it were shorthand for two other words. Throughout this book we have explored the peculiar thinking about the special status of the Bible which allowed the Rabbis leeway for these seemingly bizarre "flights" of hermeneutics.

My particular interest here is in the first midrash found in *Genesis Rabbah,* which makes use of the Wisdom motifs of Proverbs 8 to speak about the genesis of Torah. Along the way, this midrash will "solve" the grammatical problem of the Bible's first word by the method described above, separating the first letter from the remainder of the word. Most important, this opening commentary on the opening word of Torah will show us just how much value the Rabbis attribute to Torah, in all its senses, and the prescriptive (as well as descriptive) function it serves for the architecture of the universe.

Let's listen to the early-third-century Rabbi Hoshaya of the great hellenistic metropolis of Caesarea as he delivers his homily on the subject. As you cup your ear to hear him, a note of caution: it is not at all clear that what we have is a full sermon. Since the Rabbis preached on the Sabbath, when it was forbidden to observant Jews to write, we have no accurate record of their precise words. Unlike the Church Fathers such as St. Augustine, the Rabbis could not use shorthand writers to record their speech. Nor, like St. Jerome, did they circulate edited copies of their letters to a wide public (at least we have no evidence of the Rabbis doing so until the Middle

Ages). What we may have is a sermon outline, just the bare bones of Rabbi Hoshaya's ideas, recorded merely by noting the verses of Scripture he employed in his preaching and the turns he gave them. Perhaps only the last part of this sermon resembles what Hoshaya may have said. We must attend to this quandary, for the record of the sermon dates from approximately three hundred years after its delivery.

Although the editor of *Genesis Rabbah* waited three centuries to record Hoshaya's sermon, we cannot wait any longer. Here goes:

Rabbi Hoshaya opened:

Sorry, I do have to interrupt, because translation is such a slippery task. The word "opened" carries with it many layers of meaning. First, an Opening was a form of ancient sermon which introduced the weekly Torah reading in the synagogue's lectionary cycle. The gimmick of such a sermon was to open with a verse from the latter half of the Bible, usually the Writings, and slowly wend its way back so that at the end of the sermon, and only there, did it finally quote from the opening verse of that Sabbath's Torah portion. As a homiletic trick it was delightful, for it not only challenged the listeners to figure out how the preacher was going to get from where he was to where he needed to end (a feeling modern sermon listeners have often shared), but also signaled the congregants that the sermon had actually reached its end (something many modern congregants might be grateful for—a kind of homiletic alarm clock).

But there's more to Hoshaya's "opened" than just that. He did open his homily, but he opened other things, too. He opened the verse of Scripture to a new interpretation and he opened the eyes and ears and minds of his listeners to new teachings. Finally, he may simply have opened the scroll before him, so that he might read the verse accurately, aloud. These nuances are attested in a late-first-century text about another Palestinian rabbi, Jesus. Luke 4:17 shows us Jesus opening the Book of Isaiah in order to preach. But more telling is Luke 24, when the disciples meet with the risen Jesus. In verse 31, "Their eyes were opened up so they recognized him"; in verse 32, the disciples speak of how Jesus "spoke to us in the way, as he opened up the Scriptures to us." Finally, verse 45 tells us how he "opened up their minds to understand the Scripture."

> Rabbi Hoshaya opened:
> Wisdom tells us, "I was God's nursling (*amon*), day by day was I delight" (Proverbs 8:30). Let us examine this word, *amon*, for it can mean many things. *Amon* can mean *paidagog*, *amon* can mean covered, *amon* can mean hidden, and there are those who say *amon* can mean great.
> Now for the Scriptural proofs: *Amon* can mean *paidagog*, as it is written, "As the nurse (*omayn*) carries the suckling" (Numbers 11:12).

Here again I need to interrupt and explain how this "proof" worked. Both the word "nursling" in Proverbs 8:30 and the word "nurse" in Numbers share a common Semitic three-letter root form: *aleph, mem, nun*. Shifting the vowels can produce *amon* for nurseling or *omayn* for nurse. For that matter, it is the same set of letters that yields *amen*, which means truly, faithfully and all the things it does in English. As we have repeatedly seen, when a word is found in two verses of Scripture, so long as it shares the same consonantal root, it can be adduced as an equivalent for the sake of "proof." Since the voweling of words can produce some startling lexical changes, the Rabbis can rely on this device for some very creative "proof-texting."

One word here which does *not* mean the same thing as its English cognate is *paidagog,* so it, too, must be explained. In late antiquity, everyone who was anyone owned slaves. Then as now was an age of specialization, and slaves were often assigned very specific tasks, some disagreeable, some cushy. In a family with small children there was a slave assigned to be *paidagog,* which literally translates as the one who brings the child. This was the car-pool slave, as it were.

The importance of this slave is not to be dismissed, but must be placed in its context in the Roman world. Streets were unpaved and narrow, which made traffic acutely congested. To solve the traffic problem, large cities often banned vehicles during daylight hours (shades of modernity). This created yet other problems, for deliveries still had to be made on time, so the hours just before daybreak were the busiest traffic hours of the day. Imagine animal-drawn carts, no headlights (no streetlights, either, for that matter—in antiquity when it was dark, it was *dark*), drivers cursing one another, one hand on the whip, the other holding a torch so they could see. Deliveries are jostling in the back of the carts, cinders flying, and for good measure, let's have it rain so the streets are thick with mud.

It is at this moment that the six-year-old darling of the household emerges into the dark street to make his way to the shopfront that serves as his elementary-school classroom. He has to be there by sunrise, for in a world with no electricity, every moment of daylight is engaged. It is no wonder that the family specifies a slave to accompany the child to the classroom and home to assure his safety. Now, if the slave was smart, he hung around in the back of the class and learned his *alphabeta* as well, for a literate slave is worth more to his master than an illiterate. And when the precious boy came home, the slave might be able to tutor him in his lessons (hence our modern pedagogue). But for our sake, we need only to remember the narrow muddy streets to envision the slave carrying his charge to his destination.

How poignant is Rabbi Hoshaya's proof-text, for the quotation from Numbers has Moses speaking to God, complaining about the responsibilities he's been saddled with toward the sinful people Israel. Moses kvetches, Shall I carry them, then, like a *paidagog*? In that moment the third-century congregation sees Moses, giver of the Torah, as a lowly slave, literally carrying his charges to and fro. But the same image captures the vision of Moses as the tutor, laboriously teaching the recalcitrant Israelites to read the Book. The picture is sufficiently complete that one wonders if Hoshaya needed to say any more than the outline already quoted. But let's listen to more of his sermon:

> *Amon* can mean covered, as it is written, "They who were covered (*emunim*) in scarlet" (Lamentations 4:5).

Here I won't even quibble with Rabbi Hoshaya that the verse actually means "they who were raised to the scarlet." Whether they are actually wearing the cloak of the ruler or are figuratively meant to wear it makes little difference. The point of the proof when quoted in full remains the same—the people Israel sinned and now are fallen low. Perhaps, if we wished to flesh out the sermon, we might homilize that had they studied Torah, which is the truest form of "wearing scarlet," perhaps they would not have been exiled. But that is my sermon and not necessarily Hoshaya's, so let's again return to him:

> *Amon* can mean hidden, as it is written, "Mordecai hid (*omayn*) Hadassah" (Esther 2:7).

For this proof-text Hoshaya deserves the prove-a-midrash-with-another-midrash award, since no translation renders this verse quite as Hoshaya would have it. Almost every text translates it something like "Mordecai raised Hadassah." So, we may ask, how did Rabbi Hoshaya get to his creative reading of *amon* equals *omayn* which means hidden? Well, there's a story here.

Esther, a.k.a. Hadassah, was born a beautiful Jewish baby girl and raised by her uncle Mordecai (which is what the verse of Esther means to tell us). The midrash carries on: When Uncle Mordecai saw how beautiful Hadassah/Esther was, he vowed to hide her away (remember Abraham and Sarah at the Egyptian border?) lest the gentiles see her and one of them take her away as his wife. God beneficently kept her from view until which time King Ahasuerus had his infamous beauty contest. We all know how that story ends: Mordecai enters his niece Esther in the contest, she wins, gets to marry a gentile after all, but this time it saves the Jewish people! No doubt Rabbi Hoshaya's audience appreciated his joking proof, tipped off, as we are not, by his broad wink to the congregation. One last proof remains from this part of our Rabbi's sermon, and it's the most farfetched of them yet.

> *Amon* can mean great, as it is written, "Are you not better than Noh-Amon?" (Nahum 3:8).

Here Hoshaya has *amon* on both sides of the biblical equation, but he is lacking "great." Never fear, Hoshaya has an ace up his sleeve:

> Of course, translated into Aramaic this verse reads, "Are you not better than Alexandria, the great [city]?"

Here Hoshaya has simply (and outrageously) extended his "equation." Now he no longer proves one verse's meaning in Scripture from another, he proves one meaning from the oral Aramaic translation of another verse—even by rabbinic lights stretching an already thin concept of "proof." The verse from the biblical prophet Nahum has a city called Noh-Amon. Noh must equal Alexandria, so Amon must equal great. Wow, it works, but is that allowed? That is, no doubt, what Hoshaya's congregants asked themselves as they saw the degree to which he was prepared to bend biblical lexicography for the sake of his homily.

What might Rabbi Hoshaya have answered? Probably nothing. This was, after all, homiletics. It was entertainment. It was not binding on anyone, it was no one's dogma. It was a sermon, meant to offer didactic instruction in a lighthearted fashion. Of course, we may well lack the thesis of Rabbi Hoshaya's lesson. Did he suggest that Torah is hidden, but if diligently studied can be brought into the light so that it and its students will be seen to be great? We'll never know. But let's recap the homily so far before we go on to part five, which finally addresses the opening verse of Genesis:

> Rabbi Hoshaya opened, Wisdom tells us, "I was God's nursling (*amon*), day by day was I delight" (Proverbs 8:30). Let us examine this word, *amon,* for it can mean many things. *Amon* can

mean *paidagog*, *amon* can mean covered, *amon* can mean hidden, and there are those who say *amon* can mean great. Now for the Scriptural proofs: *Amon* can mean *paidagog*, as it is written, "As the nurse (*omayn*) carries the suckling" (Numbers 11:12). *Amon* can mean covered, as it is written, "They who were covered (*emunim*) in scarlet" (Lamentations 4:5). *Amon* can mean hidden, as it is written, "Mordecai hid (*omayn*) Hadassah" (Esther 2:7). *Amon* can mean great, as it is written, "Are you not better than Noh-Amon?" (Nahum 3:8). Of course, translated into Aramaic this verse reads, "Are you not better than Alexandria, the great?"

Now, it is time for Rabbi Hoshaya to come home to his point and teach us about the grammatical difficulty in the first word of Genesis, to show us the importance of midrash for the interpretation of Scripture (which they are just beginning to read through anew yet once again in his synagogue), and to draft the importance of the Torah for the architecture of the universe. His sermon resumes:

Another interpretation: *Amon* can mean artisan (*uman*). The Torah said, I was the artisan's tool of the Holy, praised be He. It is the way of the world that when a king builds a palace, he does not build it himself, but hires an architect, and the architect doesn't just build it straight out of his head, but has scrolls (*diphthera*) and tablets (*pinaks*) so he may know how to place the rooms and doors.

Here Rabbi Hoshaya has shifted gears as he begins to bring his homily to its close. He does not invoke another linguistic proof asserting that the word in Proverbs 8:30 means something new, but instead takes advantage of the context of that chapter. As mentioned above, Wisdom speaks at that juncture of the Bible; hypostatized into a concrete, almost cartoon-character form, she tells us of her origins. For Rabbi Hoshaya, this is none other than Torah herself speaking. She tells us how she preexisted the creation of the universe. Indeed, she proudly informs us that it was she who served as God's blueprint for creation. No longer are we to understand the opening chapter of Genesis as Torah, descriptive of past creation, we must now understand it as prescriptive.

Hoshaya shifts, as well, to a cosmology familiar to his congregants. There are elements of Platonic thought in his description of how first the idea comes to mind, then the plans, and only then the concrete creation of the palace. From God's thought comes Torah which serves as the blueprint for the universe. There is a subtle polemic here, for many detractors of ancient Judaism saw the laws of the Bible, particularly Sabbath rest, as unnatural. Rabbi Hoshaya seems to say that nothing could be more natural than the law of the Torah, it is the very foundation of all existence.

Before we turn to Rabbi Hoshaya's peroration which brings his sermon to completion, let's also note his parable. He indicates a rabbinic *mashal* by his invocation: It is the way of the world. This is a sophisticated device in rabbinic preaching, most often used in conjunction with a human king. As we will see later, this king is contrasted with the King of the King of Kings—God. Sometimes God turns out to do just the opposite of a human monarch. More often, God is compared in one-to-one correspondence, the point of the parable being to teach some otherwise abstruse piece of theology in *concrete* terms.

Hoshaya invokes a king who uses an architect with scrolls and tablets. We need to jump back to Hoshaya's time to understand the function of these tools, and so the delicious nuances of his preaching. Thanks to works preserved in Greek and Latin, we know a good deal about architectural theory in the Roman world. Even today, works like Vitruvius's *On Architecture* are used to describe how harmony in architecture must be of a piece with its surroundings. Harmony in a building mirrors harmony in the cosmos. So the imagery of architecture is germane to our passage of Scripture.

Material remains of late antiquity show us, as well, how architects actually went about building. Their practice roughly parallels modern practice—blueprints are drawn up in an office to lay out the broad lines of the building (rooms and doors) and more detail is added for the sake of depositing the plans in the city archives. On site, however, a second set of working drawings is needed to account for variations in topography, materials delivered, the capabilities of the workers and the like. So, as in the rabbinic *mashal*-parable, the architect uses both scrolls and tablets.

Books were always written on scrolls. Such scrolls were expensive, permanent records. They were written on parchment, made of specially prepared animal skins. It was difficult to erase from such a parchment, so only formal volumes were kept that way, for library usage. More ephemeral works were kept on tablets. These were wooden frames with hard wax surfaces. The wax was inscribed with a stylus and could be erased with the side of the fist. In the architectural trade, blueprints meant for filing in the archives were written on parchment (Greek: *diphthera*). On-site working drawings were made on the ubiquitous wax tablets (Greek: *pinaks*). Rabbi Hoshaya has accurately captured the practice of architects in his day.

But scrolls and tablets had other meanings for the late-antique mind, as well. For instance, Greek and Latin classics were, as mentioned above, always written on parchment scrolls. Jewish books which were designated for ritual use, such as a Torah scroll, also had to be written on parchment. In fact, when the Mishnah describes what makes a Torah scroll "kosher," it borrows the Greek term *diphthera* to describe the finished parchment. Intriguingly, early Christian books were written on tablets. One could string a number of tablets together into a diptych or a triptych, or even larger. When these strings of tablets shifted from wood and wax to papyrus quires, the modern codex (a bound book, like the one you're holding) was born. So Christians get credit for bringing the codex into popular use, while Jews get credit for retaining the classical form of book preparation.

But even within the Jewish world, books took two forms. We have seen above that there was a distinction in the rabbinic world between the written Torah and the Oral Torah. The written Torah, as just mentioned, was preserved on a parchment scroll. The Oral Torah was meant to be oral—recited by teacher to disciple. But students will always be students; they will urgently want to take notes, to write down memory aids to keep all of the jumble of oral interpretations of Scripture and Mishnah in order. Though the teachers were zealous about their distinction between written and oral Torah, they allowed their students to take notes on an ephemeral medium, the wax tablet. Perhaps they thought that this was the closest thing to oral that written could come—since a wave of the hand could erase the oral text. So for the members of Rabbi Hoshaya's world the scrolls and tablets of the architect carried a second, perhaps weightier valence—an allusion to the means of preserving the written and oral Torahs.

Now that we've filled in all the background of late-antique realia and know what the drafting rooms and libraries looked like, we can return to Rabbi Hoshaya and allow him the courtesy of finishing his sermon:

> Thus [like the architect looking at his plans] did the Holy, praised be He, look into the Torah and create the universe. So the Torah states: "*Be-resheet,* By means of (*be*) Beginning (*resheet*) God created . . ." (Genesis 1:1), and the word "Beginning" here refers to the Torah, of which it is written, "God created me the Beginning of his ways" (Proverbs 8:22).

How deftly does Hoshaya step around the "When the beginning . . ." dilemma. Rather than take a stand on translating one way or another, Rabbi Hoshaya chooses the third option and turns the knotty word into something else entirely. By separating the initial letter from the rest of the word, Rabbi Hoshaya makes the text mean something new. Now, the verse refers to agency—by means of something God created everything else. What was that something? Why, *resheet.* Using the same type of linguistic equations he used earlier, Rabbi Hoshaya invokes another verse to tell us what that *resheet* was. It was Torah, speaking in the book of Proverbs 8 as Wisdom, telling about her premundane origins. Now Torah, who is Lady Wisdom and no other, can speak to Hoshaya's audience as she tells of her role as God's blueprint for creation. All in all, a rather respectful introduction to the first verse of the Bible.

Hoshaya's sermon betrays a great deal about rabbinic attitudes toward the Torah in late antiquity. It was a Book which demanded special hermeneutics and could bear an interpretive scrutiny which no other work could carry. It was there before the universe, indeed—the blueprint for all existence was to be found therein. The seeming cruxes of grammar and the like are not problems at all, they are opportunities to delve into the deeper meanings of the Torah's wisdom. By concentrating on the hard parts, difficult lessons are learned with clarity. The creation of the universe is consonant with the best of late-antique science, as the Rabbis knew it. They present a Platonic cosmology that bridges the gap between God as orderer of the universe and God as creator *ex nihilo*. In short, as a brief and stunning introduction to the Torah as the Rabbis read it, Hoshaya's homily ties up all the loose ends.

But there remains for this modern writer one nagging loose end which Rabbi Hoshaya did not explicitly address. Since I think that he and his audience implicitly understood it, allow me to raise the problem and its solution. I wrote above of how the Rabbis use the *mashal*-parable to illustrate in concrete terms what would otherwise be abstruse points of theology. The tendency among these *mashal*-parables is toward congruence—that is, there is one-to-one correspondence between the parable and the point of theology being illustrated. So, for instance, if the parable has five points, we might expect five lessons to be drawn in the "moral" (*nimshal*) to the parable.

This is what nags me about Hoshaya's example: in his *mashal* he has his architect looking into both scrolls (*diphthera*) and tablets (*pinaks*) to determine how to build his palace. Yet, when the sermon draws to a close, God looks only into the Torah to learn how to build the universe. Where is the congruence? Where is the one-to-one correspondence? I suggest that for his rabbinic audience, Hoshaya's point was clearer left implicit than had he verbalized it. For him, God did use two sets of plans to create the universe. The one explicitly mentioned was the one which lay before Hoshaya on the reader's platform: the written Torah, on its parchment (*diphthera*). Unmentioned precisely because it was not meant to be written, but palpably present in the minds of every listener in the room thanks to generations of notes on wax tablets (*pinaks*) was God's other set of instructions for the creation of the universe, the oral Torah. Like the working drawings of the architect, it was oral interpretation which brought the written document in line with the topography, the materials delivered and the capabilities of the workers.

For Rabbi Hoshaya and his rabbinic colleagues, it could not be otherwise. Without the interpretation of Scripture, there could be no universe.

Chapter Twelve

READING THE BOOK

· ·

Turn it, turn it, round and round
In it all things can be found.

This aphorism is attributed to an otherwise unknown sage with the unlikely name of Ben Bag Bag. The lyrics of his ditty lucidly capture rabbinic faith in the power of scriptural exegesis. The Rabbis and their disciples made the Bible a timeless text precisely because they believed that if they turned it and returned to it, if they engaged it in dialogue, the Tanakh could offer the answers to their questions. Everything *was* in it, provided one understood just how to read it. By now we've seen enough of the ways in which the Rabbis read the Book to understand that their presumptions about its continuously revelatory power were enforced by the muscle of their exegetical ingenuity.

Most probably by now, *your* Bible has come down off the shelf and been thoroughly thumbed, if for no other reason than to answer the incredulous question, "Does it really say that?" In choosing to review pentateuchal narratives about creation, faith, anthropology, theodicy, sexuality, parent-child relations and sibling rivalries, we've challenged fundamental assumptions about the biblical worldview.

The point here is not only to undermine a way of reading the Bible which renders it useless for the modern world and so keeps it on the shelf, but to illuminate some of the processes by which one religious community has forced the text to speak to the various elements in its Weltanschauung. My not so hidden message is that communal study of the Bible, even now, can continue to provide us with a means for clarifying our ideas about the world around us and for linking them historically to a long-standing tradition. Bible study along these lines not only serves the various religious communities which undertake it, but can even afford a springboard for secular discussion of humanistic values.

To complement my desire to see the Bible as a text for a universal range of readers, I have discussed the very particular readings of the rabbinic exegetes. I chose the Rabbis because they were nonfundamentalist in their approach and came to the text with very few preconditions for finding their agenda. Their long and interactive history of reading the Book makes them thoroughly appropriate guides in helping us experience their methods of earning profit from reading Scripture. We have seen how they use the Bible to help form community and how their community informs their reading of the Bible.

As *this* book draws to a conclusion, it is worthwhile to examine whether the reading strategies of the Rabbis can be of use to us today in our encounter with Scripture (or any other text). Some of their hermeneutic methods will be immediately appealing, some completely inappropriate for our needs. Since the sages quoted in this volume cover a time span of approximately one thousand years and a geographic distribution stretching from Narbonne in southern France to Babylonia (modern Iraq and Iran), it's apposite to summarize the broad range of techniques they employ.

In the pages that follow I group these hermeneutic norms and assumptions into categories which help us better judge their usefulness today. Some of the examples will recapitulate passages we've studied earlier in this book, others will be new. Needless to say, many other methods are employed and recorded in the broad corpus of rabbinic literature, as well as in the works of the Church Fathers and other groups of biblical exegetes.

Both the Rabbis and the Church Fathers made a distinction between the simple meaning of the text (Hebrew: *peshat*) and the homiletical lesson drawn from the reading (Hebrew: *derash*). No one, however, pretends that the "simple" meaning is hard and fast for all time. The interaction of reader and Bible all but guarantees that *peshat* and *derash* are on a continuum with no clear border distinguishing them. Often what appears to be a rather farfetched narrative spun for a homily in fact captures the essence of the biblical message. But the message may change from one generation to another. The paradox of the situation was best expressed by the scholar Jose Faur when he explained that the oral Torah in fact served the function of keeping the canonical written Bible a fluid text through endless commentary and interpretation.

The notion of *canon* is very important here, for the Rabbis take the motley anthology of books that make up the Hebrew Bible and treat it as a unified document. Even as their sense of *peshat* informs them that Daniel and Genesis were written centuries apart from one another, they can quote Daniel to explicate the creation story. The principle that one verse of Scripture can illuminate another is one of the oldest, simplest and most basic means of midrash.

Another basic assumption of the midrashist invokes what the Rabbis perceived to be the divine valence of the text.

There were many, many correct readings of Scripture. Although communal consensus could determine what might be deemed an inappropriate interpretation, on the whole the Rabbis gloried in the fact that no one reading could exclusively corner a verse. In their parlance, there were at least seventy facets to each word of that highly polished gem of revelation, Torah. It was the midrashist's job to provide the right setting and the correct foil so that the truths contained therein might shine forth. Oddly enough, by removing the temptation to exclusivity, by obviating the necessity for fundamentalist authority, the Rabbis gave the Book tremendous revelatory power. Freed from the constraints of finding one correct interpretation, they uncovered the infinite truths intended by the Infinite Author of the text.

This is a fundamental difference between the rabbinic approach to Scripture and the most extreme waves of postmodern literary criticism. The Rabbis were firm believers in Authorial intent: everything they said had been revealed at Sinai long ago. Even those sages who shared the view of the school of Rabbi Ishmael—that the Torah could be treated like normal human discourse—shared the belief in the divine authority imbued in Scripture. Even as they debated the very human circumstances of the Bible's authorship, the sages shared the assumption that it somehow revealed God's will. This was poignantly expressed in the twentieth century by the great rabbi Louis Finkelstein who said, "When I pray I talk to God. When I study God talks to me."

For the Rabbis there were many ways to hear God talk, as it were, and many means of finding revelation in the words they studied. Like the hellenistic exegetes around them, the Rabbis relied on allegory to wrench contemporary meaning from the text. "This," they could tell you, "means That." The beauty of allegory is that there need not be any correspondence between the words on parchment and what the interpreter said they meant. This was true not only for the Rabbis, but also for the typological interpretations of the Bible found in the New Testament and the Dead Sea Scrolls. As with the psychoanalyst interpreting dreams, it was the act of interpretation that brought redemption.

The parallel to dream interpretation is apt. The Rabbis themselves explicitly acknowledged that the techniques were the same (in one delightful legend, the Rabbis have a dreamer offer a verse of Scripture as the content of his dream). The dreamlike quality of exegesis also allowed the Rabbis to deconstruct the context of a biblical passage and atomize the various verses of Scripture in order to learn their didactic lessons. While removing a verse from its context is anathema to modern critics of the Bible, it was standard operating procedure to the exegetes of late antiquity.

There is yet another area of basic asumption where the Rabbis stand apart from the modern critics. Both sets of exegetes recognize the moral dilemmas that the biblical characters present to the reader. Modern critics tend to let them stand, identify them, even revel in them (as I did in the chapter about Abraham and Sarah). The Rabbis prefer to solve the dilemmas. Whether by whitewashing or by retelling the tale or by shifting the blame, the Rabbis prefer not to leave moral loose ends. Their tendency to tidy up and offer balance to the lives of the patriarchs and matriarchs should be understood as more than a manifestation of discomfort with a different moral climate: it was a hermeneutic principle.

Some of the Rabbis' more specific hermeneutic methods seem far removed from modern strategies of reading. We mentioned that the Rabbis were prepared to atomize the text and take a verse of Scripture out of context. They are also capable of atomizing to the point that an individual word— or, on occasion, even an individual letter—can be lifted from a verse for didactic profit. This practice stems from the hermeneutic assumption, which certain Church Fathers shared, that there is nothing superfluous in Scripture. Thus every word, even if seemingly extraneous, may be used for homiletical ends.

Similarly, the Rabbis can take a word of the Bible and break it into parts, as though it were shorthand for something else. This is roughly akin to reading a headline which has the name of our president in it and assuming that BUSH is actually an abbreviation for BULL SH— Well, you get the idea. As a modern method of reading it simply doesn't wash. Equally bizarre from our perspective is the ancient habit of assigning numerical equivalents to letters, hence to words, yielding a sum for every part of Scripture. The equivalencies "discovered" through the hellenistic method of gematria was used by rhetors, Rabbis and Church Fathers alike, but only cryptographers find any use for the method in our century.

This rabbinic focus on individual words plays itself out in the attention they pay to the lexicographic range of biblical Hebrew. We saw in the last chapter how their survey of the root *aleph, mem, nun* provided the impetus for a sermon. Equally, the Rabbis can take a descriptive word quite literally with startling effect. Their notion of macrocosmic Adam is but one example of reading too literally in order to extract a point.

All of these examples underscore a pleasure of the Rabbis' exegesis, which is their irrepressible love of puns. Time and again, whenever they have the opportunity, one groaner after another moves their homilies along. They use these verbal equivalents to equate verses, too. If a word means something in one verse, it should have similar meaning in another verse. So far so good. The Rabbis carry this to an extreme method of exegesis by assuming that if two verses have a word in common, the very content of the verses must be similar! This is equivalent to saying that any sentence in this book which has the word "of" in it must be talking about the same matter as any other sentence with an "of." Even the Rabbis recognized the absurdities this particular exegetical technique could raise, so they severely limited its application in rendering legal decisions. It remained their assumption, however, that for the sake of a good homily, anything goes.

While we, for instance, would not argue from silence, the Rabbis regularly employed the technique in both homiletical and legal exegeses. I offer an example of how the Rabbis reason using this method taught to me by my friend Rabbi Richard Levine. Imagine someone coming home from a Long Island wedding. When asked to comment on the affair they state, "Oh, the bride was beautiful, the groom was so happy!" From this rapturous description one infers, of course, that the bride was crying her eyes out and the groom looked like a gorilla. This is how a midrashist uses silence to homiletic advantage.

Midrashists also loved to employ anachronism to illustrate the biblical passages they were teaching. The technique could be as subtle as referring to Moses as "our Rabbi," or more mundane, such as explaining that a *paidagog* was the slave who drove car pool. The technique also allowed the Rabbis to borrow scenes from one part of the Bible and replay them somewhere else, as in the case of Nimrod throwing Abraham into Daniel's fiery furnace. Finally, anachronism plays itself out physically when the Rabbis assume that the juxtaposition of verses or paragraphs of Scripture teaches us something of time sequence. This was the means by which the Rabbis determined Isaac's age at the time of the Aqedah, by reference to Sarah's age at her death as reported in the following section of Scripture. Juxtapositions can also be used to infer other forms of causality, such as the reason Aaron's sons died ("Do not drink wine or liquor").

The death of Aaron's two sons also showed us an old rabbinic technique for harmonizing apparently contradictory passages of the Bible. When two verses disagree, bring a third verse to tip the balance—"They offered strange fire"—a method we also saw used to determine how Adam and Eve were created.

Contradictory verses are also explained away by historicizing, much as modern Bible scholars would do. "Beat your swords into plowshares" was prophesied at a time of peace. "Beat your plowshares into swords" was prophesied in another era, at a time of war. On the whole, both modern and ancient readers resort to finding the background setting to explicate the text.

We have also seen how the Rabbis (and Jesus, while we're at it) repeatedly employed parables to make their points of theology, and that these parables tended to be concrete examples taken from daily life. This use of palpable reality to illustrate the world of ideas made their listeners much more comfortable in dealing with the abstract. As with the rest of the hellenistic world, the Rabbis loved folk tales and fables, and freely adapted them to teach their own particular lessons.

Another technique used in the hellenistic world (and ours, too) was reasoning from minor to major premise. This method is ubiquitous in rabbinic literature, but is not without its dangers. My teacher, Israel Francus, once illustrated how even such a simple hermeneutic norm as this could be abused. "I can take money from my wallet and you can take money from your wallet," he began, "but you cannot take money from my wallet." Then he reasoned from minor to major premise: "If you, who cannot take money from my wallet, can take money from your wallet, how much the more so is it permissible for me, who *can* take money from my wallet, to take money from your wallet!" Another triumph of rabbinic logic.

While we're still puzzling over how Professor Francus opened my wallet, let us run through a quick list of other methods the Rabbis employed. First, they loved to make lists —like Abraham's ten trials, or the Ten Tribes of Israel (go count them) or even the Ten Commandments (Jews and Christians count them differently, but they are mentioned as a group of ten in the Book of Deuteronomy, so we can't blame the Rabbis or Church Fathers for this confusion). Along these lines the Rabbis also liked to make lists of sets, like those who made inappropriate requests of God (Eliezer, Jeptha, Dopey, Sneezy and Bashful).

Mention of Eliezer, Abraham's slave who told and retold the tale of his quest for a wife for young Isaac, reminds me of the rabbinic penchant for expanding narratives of the Bible. Sometimes they expand the plot, sometimes they add dialogue, sometimes they flesh out the characters more, often accomplishing this by identifying otherwise anonymous characters with ones we already know (like Eliezer with the anonymous slave of Genesis 24).

One means of expanding the narrative is assuming the point of view of an otherwise minor character in a given scene (like Sarah in the Aqedah, or Billy Bathgate, for that matter). These techniques find their fullest expression in the early Middle Ages when narrative retelling of the Bible (as in *Pirke Rabbi Eliezer*) and expansive translations called *Targum* were all the rage in the synagogue. The dialogues invented for Isaac, Ishmael and Eliezer surrounding the retelling of the Aqedah offer a sterling example of this hermeneutic method.

They also reflect the rabbinic principle that the behaviors of the children reflect the lives of their parents, as is also the case with Isaac's descent into Egypt with his wife. This repetition of plot devices for the various patriarchs and matriarchs is a reminder that these individual characters serve as eponymous ancestors—they represent the history of the nation as a whole. Thus, it is necessary for descent into Egypt to be a prototypical scene in the patriarchal narratives, just as it is the standard myth that holds the central place in the imagined history of the people.

Two last techniques round out this list of forty (now isn't that a nice biblical number) hermeneutic methods illustrated in this book. The first was employed extensively in the rabbinic treatment of Moses' death, and is a standard technique of modern (but not postmodern) literary criticism. The psychological reading of the narrative (in our case, the stages Moses and Israel went through to prepare for his death) allowed the Rabbis a powerful tool for offering consolation to their emotionally needy congregants. This enabled the Rabbis to preserve their theology even as they suggested a role which God could play in helping mourners and people otherwise bereaved.

The second technique, an even greater staple of their theology and its concomitant hermeneutic was *lex talionis,* or measure for measure. Again and again the Rabbis reassured those who sought their advice that God rewarded and punished measure for measure. As often as was necessary they read the

Bible through this lens in order to confirm their belief in a just and merciful God who created a world full of blessings.

The broad range of methods here surveyed point to an uncanny ability the Rabbis had at getting behind the biblical text, reading the words, the lines and between the lines until they finally got the point. Even their wackiest exegeses never lost sight of the message of Scripture, and they transmitted this message in every way that they saw fit. But what of us? Can we still read the Bible for profit? Is there a moral lesson yet for us? Can we use Scripture as a source of twenty-first-century ethics? Is there even intellectual pleasure to be gained from the reading of such an ancient and arcane document?

My answer is a resounding yes. Beyond what the Rabbis have taught us, we have the means at our disposal to make reading the Book a pleasurable and meaningful exercise. There are only two prerequisites for reading the Book profitably. First, I believe it is necessary to do so with a community. Now, a community may be one partner, a church or synagogue study group, your bowling team or the computer operator at work. Gather your group and set a fixed time to read together. Don't say you'll do it when you have spare time—you may not find that time. Rather, set a time, be it once a day, once a week, even once a month (less often than that allows no continuity), and stick to that time religiously. In fact, about the only things that need be religious in your reading of the Bible are the requirement for your group to meet regularly and a second, more difficult demand.

This second prerequisite is an open mind. Each of us comes to the Bible with a bias. It may be rebellion against the religious instruction of our youth, it may be the doctrines our synagogue or church imposes upon us. It may be the college we went to, it may be the city we live in or the baseball team we follow (speaking of religious devotion). Know in advance that you open the Book with bias and prejudice. It is extremely important to realize that every time you've ever read the Bible you read it as midrash, and are likely to continue to do so forevermore. But reading the Bible like any other book allows you to begin to see your biases and understand what you have at stake as you read it.

It is for this reason that I recommend that all interpretations be given a hearing. It doesn't matter whether the reading of Scripture is traditional or modern, fundamentalist or critical, Christian or Muslim or Jewish, whether it comes from an adult or a child, an agnostic or a believer, a professor or a cab driver. Every group, every person has something unique to offer in the interpretation of the Bible—all we need to do is learn how to listen. Different points of view expand our abilities to hear the nuances of the text, different kinds of hermeneutics allow us to make new discoveries every time we read together.

To further this end I recommend that when your study group reads together, you avail yourselves of as many different translations of the biblical text as you can garner. If you read Hebrew, well and good, but translations still have a lot to teach you. If you have access to other languages (German, Spanish and so on), even better. You can find Bible translations in just about any language you can muster. The more translations, the more interpretations you will learn.

The importance of open-minded study was long ago recognized by the Rabbis when they declared that Torah study was a commandment demanded by God. Rabbi David Halivni, Columbia University professor of Talmud, is fond of pointing out that the commandment is fulfilled whether or not you get the "right" interpretation of a passage. The commandment is to study—there is no one right answer. Because of this, everyone's opinion must be heard.

I am very fortunate to be part of a monthly study group under the auspices of the Jewish Theological Seminary in New York. For four years now we have studied the Book of Genesis (we read slowly). The group includes both Jewish and Gentile Bible scholars, who work hard to keep us moored to the current critical interpretations of the narratives we enjoy together. But most of the group—we average about twenty participants per session—are writers. The group (also religiously diverse) includes essayists, film critics, screenwriters, translators, poets, editors and novelists. This mixture of great readers has left me floating with excitement every month we've met. I always learn something new about the Book of Genesis and, more important, I always learn something new *from* the Book of Genesis, thanks to my colleagues, who are willing to take a risk and expose themselves a bit in order to learn.

I remember early on in our study together when fiction writer Max Apple commented on God's command to Abraham in Genesis 12. God says, "Go from your land and your birthplace and your father's house to the land I will show you. I will make you a great nation. . . ." Apple commented, before he could stop himself, "I wouldn't have written it that way!" He then sheepishly explained that God gives it all away at the outset—it is no test of Abraham's faith if he's promised a reward from the very start. What Apple said was of course true, and a valuable commentary on the scriptural passage. More important, and an icebreaker for our group, was his impulsive "I wouldn't have written it that way." In essence, it is the statement of every exegete. As soon as a commentator notices an extraneous word, or a grammati-

cal crux or a moral difficulty, he or she is saying the same
thing as Max Apple. It is with that statement that commentary begins, so we must overcome our sheepishness and realize
that to profit from the Bible we must be bold enough to
challenge the text with our intellect. For those who have
religious qualms about this approach I need only remind you
that it was God who endowed you with that intellect, so use
it to God's glory.

There are other ways of approaching the text, of bringing
our personal insights to it that help it yield its treasures to us.
Once, film critic Marcia Pally commented on the repetitious
storytelling of Abraham's slave who had brought home Rebecca as wife to Isaac, by likening it to the ways in which her
mother would repeat the qualifications of an available bache-
lor to her, then to her father and again to her aunt Faigie. Her
point was that constant repetition was a method of trying to
bring an event (marrying off her single daughter) to fruition.
.Even as we chuckled at her Jewish mother routine, we realized that Pally had put her finger on the essential narrative
technique played out in Genesis. We could understand it as
family drama because we all live through it. Genesis comments on our lives and relationships even as they help us
understand the lessons of the biblical text.

When our Genesis Seminar began to study the passages
relating to Jacob's sons, we all noticed that the narrative nar-
rowed and began more and more to treat the characters as a
tribal unit, as forebears of a nation and less as individuals. I
asked aloud what we would have if each of Jacob's twelve
sons had received the same extensive narrative treatment ac-
corded to Joseph. Writer Cynthia Ozick quipped that what
we would have was Thomas Mann's *Joseph and His Brothers.*
We all laughed as we thought of the four long volumes that

make up Mann's massive novel, but we also realized that it is in such imagination that midrash finds its way to teach the truths of the Bible's narratives. The expansion of narrative, taking a minor character's point of view, identifying anonymous figures in the text are all methods shared by midrash, Mann and many more. Margaret Atwood's powerful *A Handmaid's Tale* is but one of many works that spring to mind which employ a biblical motif in the service of modern fiction. We should not lose sight, however, of the ways in which these modern fictions shed light on the biblical narratives and cause them once again to shed sparks of insight and revelation.

I remember when we were reading the story of Joseph and I was taking advantage of Robert Benton's participation in the group. Since Benton is an accomplished screenwriter and film director (*Bonnie and Clyde, Kramer vs. Kramer, Places in the Heart*), I asked him whom he would pick for the part of Mrs. Potiphar, the mistress who tried to seduce Joseph. "Who, Robert, do you cast in the part of the femme fatale? Will it be Meryl Streep or Glenn Close?" While Benton pondered the choice, novelist Nessa Rapoport called out, "No, *Joseph* is the femme fatale."

This is a stunning insight as well as wicked humor. We all can imagine Meryl Streep in her most demanding role yet (and she gets to talk in a foreign accent)—Joseph. But the comment showed us something about Joseph, that beautiful boy who attracts women and men alike. It pointed to the metaphysical quality that accompanies God's favor and leaves us uneasy, unable to categorize such a one. The exchange in the Genesis Seminar reminded us all how uncanny the Bible often is, drawing characters who are larger than life, but who teach us the lessons we need to learn.

Quite simply it is a two-way process. We bring our insights to illuminate the Bible and the more we do so, the more the text of Scripture illuminates our lives. The pleasures and insights of reading in community not only give each individual profit from that encounter but offer the gift of community as a necessary concomitant. In laughter and amazement we discover that most precious hidden aspect of the biblical text—ourselves.

The very first rabbinic legend I quoted in this book was a story of the sage Hillel and his encounter with someone who wished to learn to read the Bible. I want to close this book with another, more famous story about Hillel and a would-be student of Scripture:

> A certain gentile came to the sage Shammai and challenged him, "Convert me, but only on the condition that you can teach me the entire Torah while I stand on one foot." Shammai pushed him away with the builder's cubit in his hand.
>
> When that same man came to Hillel, he converted him. Hillel told him, "Don't do anything to a friend that you hate yourself." Hillel continued, "This is the entire Torah, everything else is commentary. Go now. Study."

CPSIA information can be obtained at www.ICGtesting.com
Printed in the USA
BVOW021457130112

280443BV00001B/4/A

9 780827 607866